ASSESSOR WORKBOOK

Guidance and practice in vocational assessment

Chris Cook

Consultant editor: George Barr

MACMILLAN

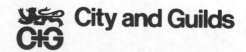

City and Guilds

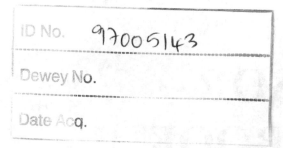

First published 1994 by
THE MACMILLAN PRESS LTD
Houndmills, Basingstoke, Hampshire RG21 2XS
and London
Companies and representatives
throughout the world

ISBN 0-333-60103-3

A catalogue record for this book is available
from the British Library

Printed in Great Britain by Unwin Brothers Ltd,
The Gresham Press, Old Woking, Surrey.
A member of Martins Printing Group

Acknowledgements
Thanks are due to the following for help and advice received at various stages in the development of the text:
Simon Allison, City and Guilds; Lesley Hebron, Barton Consultancy Services; and Claire Vaughan, Claire Vaughan Associates. Trainee assessors on my training courses have contributed many good ideas and clarified my thinking by their questions.
The author and publishers thank HMSO for permission to reproduce extracts from the TDLB standards in Appendix 1.

ASSESSOR WORKBOOK

City and Guilds Co-publishing Series

City and Guilds of London Institute has a long history of providing assessments and certification to those who have undertaken education and training in a wide variety of technical subjects or occupational areas. Its business is essentially to provide an assurance that predetermined standards have been met. That activity has grown in importance over the past few years as government and national bodies strive to create the right conditions for the steady growth of a skilled and flexible workforce.

Both teachers and learners need materials to support them as they work towards the attainment of qualifications, and City and Guilds is pleased to be working with several distinguished publishers towards meeting that need. It has been closely involved in planning, author selection and text appraisal, although the opinions expressed in the publications are those of the individual authors and are not necessarily those of the Institute.

City and Guilds is fully committed to the projects listed below and is pleased to commend them to teaching staff, students and their advisers.

Carolyn Andrew and others, *Business Administration Level I* and *Business Administration Level II*, John Murray

Chris Cook, *Assessor Workbook*, Macmillan

David Minton, *Teaching Skills in Further and Adult Education*, Macmillan

Graham Morris and Lesley Reveler, *Retail Certificate Workbook* (Levels 1 and 2), Macmillan

Peter Riley (consultant editor), *Computer-aided Engineering*, and associated workbooks: *CNC Setting and Operation; CNC Part Programming; Computer-aided Draughting; Robot Technology; Programmable Logic Control; Drawing Standards for CAE*, Macmillan

Barbara Wilson, *Information Technology: The Basics*, Macmillan

Caroline Wilkinson, *Information Technology in the Office*, Macmillan

CONTENTS

INTRODUCTION

The main reference throughout the text is to NVQs.

Assessment methods and approaches are different for GNVQs in some ways. Notes are given where necessary.

This workbook is intended as a guide for those who are already assessors of vocational qualifications or are training for such a role.

Assessors come from a variety of backgrounds and bring different experiences and expertise to the role. As an assessor, you will undertake activities many of which you will already be familiar with.

The workbook is designed to cover what assessors do across a range of settings, from schools and colleges to different workplaces and training programmes. The vocational qualifications assessors will be assessing include:

○ National Vocational Qualifications (NVQs) from level 1 to level 5

○ General National Vocational Qualifications (GNVQs) at Foundation, Intermediate and Advanced levels.

Plan how best to use this workbook to meet your own needs. You may work through the book on your own, with a colleague or as part of a group.

The workbook contains the following material:

Chapters 1, 2, 3 and 13

1. **Background information on vocational qualifications and assessors.**

   This will help you put the qualification you are assessing and your assessment setting into context in the wider assessment field. Chapter 13 includes definitions of some of the words and terms you will meet.

Appendices 1 and 2

2. **Self-assessment material using national standards of assessor performance.**

   This will help you measure your present skills and knowledge, and plan what you need to learn or practise.

Chapters 4 to 10

3. **Instructional material about the process and skills of assessment, with exercises to help you apply your learning to your own situation.**

   This will help you develop your knowledge and skills as an assessor.

Chapters 11, 12 and Appendix 3

4. **Examples of the assessment process, documents, procedures and portfolio development.**

   This will give you some examples, ideas and tools that you might use or adapt as an assessor.

The workbook

The content of the workbook is linked to national standards of competence published by the Training and Development Lead Body (TDLB). It is based on two units of competence:

D32 Assess candidate performance

D33 Assess candidate using differing sources of evidence.

These two units describe assessor activities and are the national standards on which the qualifications are based for those assessing vocational qualifications.

The main aim of the workbook is to help you work towards a qualification as an assessor based on these national standards. The qualification you aim for may be based on a single unit D32 or D33, or on both units D32 and D33. Which qualification you aim for depends on the scope and context of your role as an assessor. Look at Chapter 1 and discuss with colleagues which qualification will better suit your assessor role.

The workbook can be used in a number of ways:

1. Working towards a qualification as an assessor

Read Chapter 1 and talk to colleagues to decide which units describe your role. Complete the 'self-assessment' and 'planning how to use the workbook' in Appendix 2.

> Self-assessment against the national standards for assessors, leading to a plan about how to use the workbook.

The plan you decide on may include reading chapters and completing exercises in the workbook. Select what you need from the material and go through quickly what you already know.

As you work through the book and begin your role as an assessor, you will need to build a portfolio of your competent performance, and Appendix 3 covers this. This portfolio will provide evidence of your competence as an assessor.

> Building a portfolio to show your competence as an assessor.

2. Getting an overall picture of vocational qualifications

Read Chapter 3 to appreciate the basis of assessment, and then Chapter 4 to introduce you to national standards.

Chapters 1, 2, 11 and 12 will give you ideas on what actually happens and how various roles contribute to the assessment process.

3. Beginning to develop skills and knowledge as an assessor

Use the self-assessment sheets in Appendix 2 to check your present skills and knowledge.

Look at Chapters 4 to 10 for particular assessor skills.

Use the exercises to develop and practise what you learn.

4. Finding good ideas and tools for assessment

Look at Chapters 11 and 12 which show worked examples of how a candidate goes through the assessment process.

However you decide to use the workbook, remember it is flexible and adaptable to your needs and situation.

Don't feel you have to read it from cover to cover.

You can dip into it as you require and keep it as an on-going reference.

Layout of the workbook

You will find a number of different areas in the text.

Boxes like this summarise or reference material in the text.

In the margins of the text you will see boxes to summarise points or direct you to other relevant material. These act as reminders and signposts around the workbook.

When the text is directly relevant to aspects of the TDLB standards, the box is headed TDLB STANDARDS.

TDLB STANDARDS
If the text is directly relevant to TDLB standards, the relevant elements are referenced in a box like this.

This will help you relate the TDLB standards to your learning, and recognise when evidence is produced for your portfolio. Guidance on producing a portfolio is presented in Chapter 1 and Appendix 3.

The background information is often illustrated by examples from real-life assessments.

These case studies are presented in boxes:

➥ CASE STUDIES

Learning material to develop the skills and knowledge of assessors is supported with exercises.

Space is provided in the workbook to complete these exercises:

✳ EXERCISE

Sometimes in the text you are directed to activities to be completed with other documents or in collaboration with colleagues.

These other activities are presented in TO DO boxes:

TO DO !

Guidance for building a portfolio is presented in Chapter 1 and Appendix 3.

All the exercises, activities and documents that you collect could be kept in a portfolio which will provide evidence of your learning, knowledge and skills, and contribute to your competence as an assessor.

This workbook is designed to be flexible:

O **You can dip into it at any point and go quickly through the parts you are already familiar with**

O **You can use it to self-assess your present competence**

O **You can use parts of it within the assessment process for an assessment qualification**

O **You can use it on your own or with others**

O **You can keep it as an on-going reference.**

To help you decide how to start using the workbook, look at the self-assessment and planning sheets in Appendix 2.

1. WHO ARE ASSESSORS AND WHAT DO THEY DO?

THIS CHAPTER IS ABOUT:

○ The requirements to be an assessor for NVQs and GNVQs

○ The activities that assessors carry out with candidates

○ National standards of competence for assessors and awards based on these standards

○ The need to build a portfolio to show your competent performance as an assessor.

> **TDLB STANDARDS**
>
> Although not directly related to performance criteria in D32 or D33, this chapter will help assessors appreciate their overall role

THE CHAPTER WILL HELP YOU TO:

○ See what's involved in being an assessor

○ Start to understand what you will be doing with candidates

○ Begin your development process as an assessor.

KEY POINTS

1. There will be a need for large numbers of assessors as vocational qualifications grow in importance.

2. Assessors will come from the present working population of supervisors and team leaders, and will not necessarily be teachers or trainers.

3. These assessors will be trained and assessed to new national standards of competence.

4. Assessors carry out basic guidance, planning and assessment with candidates.

5. Assessors will gain awards for their competent performance.

6. Begin a portfolio to keep evidence of what you do.

As vocational qualifications grow in importance and scope, many more people will become assessors.

You may have no teaching or training background, but that doesn't stop you being an assessor.

To be a assessor you need to:

1. Know the activities you will be assessing.

Only if you know about the activities in the standards will you be able to ask relevant questions and recognise competent performance, mistakes or good practice in a candidate's performance.

2. If possible, be in regular contact with candidates.

Because assessment takes place in the normal course of work or study, the most natural and effective assessor is one who works alongside the candidate. However, in some circumstances, assessors will come into the candidate's work situation for assessment activities.

3. Be trained and competent in vocational assessment.

This workbook aims to assist this process and to help you gain an assessment qualification.

You do not need any particular qualifications or experience to become an assessor, and people from all sorts of backgrounds and experiences will provide vocational assessment where they work. Lecturers, teachers and managers will also be involved in assessment and will need to apply their general assessment experience to vocational assessment. Margaret's experience in the following case study is typical of NVQ assessors:

➥ CASE STUDY

Margaret is the office supervisor in a department of the local council. She has worked in this department since leaving school and has risen to a supervisory position through her experience and some qualifications at a local college. Three years ago young trainees appeared in her department doing NVQs in administration. Margaret spent three days training as an assessor to carry out work-based assessment for these trainees. She had no previous experience of assessment and found the training daunting. Learning about assessment and recording has helped her understand her role in supervising staff and communicating clearly.

Since finishing the training, Margaret has also been assessing staff in the department who have registered for NVQs. With the introduction of qualifications for assessors, Margaret is gathering evidence of her assessment experience in a portfolio.

The following GNVQ case study illustrates what happened for Theresa who teaches in a school:

➥ CASE STUDY

Theresa is an experienced teacher in a comprehensive school for 11 to 18 year olds. She is teaching the art and design GNVQ programme. She has little understanding of vocational qualifications and initially found her training for D32 and D33 an irritation: after all, she had been assessing pupils and their work for many years and she wondered why she needed to do the training. However, once she started to see how the training helped her plan and design assessments and support her pupils she became enthusiastic. She realised that much of her previous experience and expertise contributed to the award.

The qualifications for assessors will ensure the quality of the assessment of NVQ and GNVQ candidates. You will be required to follow a development action plan leading to these qualifications, based on standards published by the Training and Development Lead Body (TDLB).

This workbook provides the basis of the knowledge and skills you need as an assessor and will help you decide your development plan. Two of the steps in your development plan might be your self-assessment against the TDLB standards and your planning on how to use this workbook. This process is presented in Appendix 2.

> Sheets and procedures for this self-assessment and plans to use the workbook are included in Appendix 2 and described in the Introduction.

What do assessors do?

Essentially, assessors make judgements about a candidate's competence using the performance criteria, range and any guidance in the national standards.

Making this judgement in itself requires skills and knowledge about the national standards, evidence, assessment, giving feedback and recording.

> Chapters 4 to 10 cover the skills and knowledge required to be an assessor.

Some of the activities of an assessor include:

1. Explaining the standards and assessment process to candidates.

2. Helping candidates to identify their present competence in relation to the standards.

> The TDLB units, presented opposite and in Appendix 1, relate specifically to assessor activities 2 to 7.

3. Encouraging candidates to identify and gather evidence of their competence.

4. Planning assessments, development and reviews with the candidate.

5. Assessing candidates.

6. Carrying out reviews with candidates and questioning them about assessments.

7. Making assessment decisions, giving positive and constructive feedback and completing any documentation.

Assessors will also contribute to the whole assessment team, working with internal verifiers, who are responsible for monitoring the quality of assessments, and liaising with managers and others involved in the training and assessment process.

> Other roles in the assessment team, such as internal verifiers and trainers, are described in Chapter 2.

Qualifications for assessors

The national standards for vocational assessment have been published by the TDLB. Competence in these standards will become the requirement of all those assessing in a vocational qualification system. The standards describe the performance and knowledge required of assessors. The workbook will help you to prepare to become a competent assessor. The examples, exercises and TO DO activities will help you practise your role as an assessor and develop your competence.

> If you are not sure about the content and layout of national standards, look at Chapter 4 'Explaining national standards and assessment'.

The two units for assessors are given below with their element titles; greater detail is presented in Appendix 1, giving performance criteria, range statements and guidance for each element with references to chapter and topics in the workbook.

TDLB Unit D32

UNIT TITLE: **Assess candidate performance**

ELEMENT TITLES

> These are the two units from the TDLB standards which define the standard of performance for assessors.
>
> They cover the assessor activities 2 to 7 on the previous page.

○ Agree and review a plan for assessing performance

○ Collect and judge performance evidence against criteria

○ Collect and judge knowledge evidence

○ Make assessment decision and provide feedback.

TDLB Unit D33

UNIT TITLE: **Assess candidate using differing sources of evidence**

ELEMENT TITLES

○ Agree and review an assessment plan

○ Judge evidence and provide feedback

○ Make assessment decision using differing sources of evidence and provide feedback.

These two units overlap in some activities. Unit D33 describes the assessment process from a wider view, taking account of the full range of sources of evidence. Unit D32 concentrates on two sources of evidence - observation and simple questioning. This means that collecting evidence for D33 will provide evidence for D32, and vice versa. Assessors need to be clear about the scope of their role, and concentrate on the unit or units that they need.

It is important to the National Council for Vocational Qualifications (NCVQ) and the awarding bodies offering NVQs and GNVQs that all those assessing vocational qualifications are competent in the relevant units from the TDLB standards.

A number of awarding bodies have constructed qualifications based on the TDLB units for various roles within the assessment process. Qualifications exist for assessors, advisers and verifiers.

Qualifications, based on TDLB units, are available from several awarding bodies.

City and Guilds has designed a series of competence qualifications based on the TDLB units. Qualifications for those involved in the vocational assessment process are presented in a series of awards. The qualifications designed for assessors are based on the two TDLB units D32 and D33 and are detailed below.

City and Guilds Skills Assessor award - unit D32

This award is designed for the front-line assessor carrying out assessment by observation of performance and examination of the outcomes of such performance, supported by questioning to assess underpinning knowledge and understanding. A skills assessor could be a skilled worker, supervisor, manager or college tutor.

City and Guilds qualification for assessors based on the single unit D32 from the TDLB standards.

City and Guilds Vocational Assessor award - units D32 and D33

This award is designed for a specialist assessor who will have gained considerable specific experience and have relevant qualifications. The assessments carried out by the assessor are drawn from the wide range of sources of evidence specified within NVQs in order to make assessment decisions. These sources will include judgements made by other assessors, their colleagues and the candidate. The candidate's prior achievements and performance assessments will also be used.

City and Guilds qualification for assessors based on D32 and D33 from the TDLB standards.

A vocational assessor could be a supervisor, manager, college tutor or school teacher who has a responsibility for operating assessment services in conjunction with others.

Those assessing for GNVQs will need to be competent in the activities described by the two units, D32 and D33, and therefore must gain the vocational assessor award.

Assessors for GNVQs will need the award covering the two units, D32 and D33.

Before you use the workbook, be clear about which award describes the scope of your role as an assessor. You may need to discuss this with colleagues to be sure of which award to aim for.

Gathering your evidence

Start a portfolio to keep evidence of your development as an assessor.

Appendix 3 gives details of how to do this.

Because assessors will need to be assessed as competent in these units, you should keep details, documents and examples of what you do in any study, training or practice you carry out now in preparation for your role as an assessor. The suggested method of keeping such evidence of your performance and knowledge is in a portfolio (see Appendix 3 for details and formats). In this way you will be able to produce evidence of recent performance which can be acknowledged towards the recognition of competence and the award of a qualification.

The exercises in the workbook can also be used as evidence, once you complete them.

2. PART OF THE ASSESSMENT TEAM

THIS CHAPTER IS ABOUT:

○ The part that assessors play in the wider assessment team

○ Roles in the assessment process both within and outside the assessment centre.

TDLB STANDARDS

Although not directly related to performance criteria in D32 or D33, this section will help assessors appreciate their place in the assessment team and how the different roles interact.

THE CHAPTER WILL HELP YOU TO:

○ Understand where your assessment contribution fits into the overall assessment and quality control process

○ Identify people who play other roles in the assessment process

○ Have confidence in a series of quality controls that ensure consistent and reliable judgements of competence.

KEY POINTS

1. The assessor is part of a team with the internal verifier which is responsible for consistency and reliability of judgements within an assessment centre.

2. The external verifier represents the awarding body and provides an outside, objective influence to ensure consistent quality.

As an assessor, you will first become aware of being part of a team within your own organisation or centre. This team offers assessors support, advice and quality control on their performance.

The core of the assessment team

The core team consists of assessors and internal verifiers. Groups of assessors may formally or informally discuss standards and how assessments are progressing. Sharing in this way builds confidence and ensures consistency between assessors. Internal verifiers have the responsibility to support and advise assessors and co-ordinate the assessment process. They usually arrange regular meetings at which this can be done. In addition to these support meetings, internal verifiers will be monitoring the performance of assessors in applying the correct assessment process and the assessing judgements they make. They will do this by observing assessor performance and checking documents and evidence.

The purpose of this core team is to:

O   assess candidates

O   offer support and advice to assessors

O   ensure consistency in assessment judgements

O   maintain the quality control mechanisms of the assessment centre

O   identify any problems with the standards or assessment process

O   liaise with the next levels of the assessment team (managers and those responsible for training in the organisation and the external verifier).

Support to the core team

Within the organisation the core team needs support to fulfil its assessment functions. This support comes from managers and those responsible for training.

Managers will be responsible for releasing resources, and identifying and arranging the development of competent staff.

Those responsible for training will be involved in developing the competence of candidates and liaising with assessors to make their training and instruction relevant and effective.

Managers and those responsible for training may, with assessors and internal verifiers, form an assessment management team for the centre. This assessment management team will be responsible for policy monitoring and developments at the centre. The assessment management team may consist of managers, lecturers, trainers, verifiers, assessors and, possibly, candidates.

The team's overall responsibility is to:

○ design and arrange training to develop competence

○ monitor assessment centre policy on anti-discriminatory practices and appeals

○ liaise with the awarding body on centre development issues

○ liaise with the organisation on the role of vocational assessment.

External support and monitoring

Finally, the awarding body is represented by an external verifier. His or her role is to provide support, advice and quality monitoring to the approved centre. This external verifier provides an external addition to the assessment team, bringing an outside objective influence to ensure quality.

> The external verifier from the awarding body completes the overall assessment team.

The assessment team can be represented by this diagram:

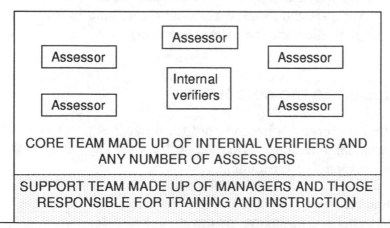

3. THE BASIS OF ASSESSMENT FOR VOCATIONAL QUALIFICATIONS

THIS CHAPTER IS ABOUT:

○ How vocational qualifications are assessed

○ Types and sources of evidence

○ The different kinds of evidence used in vocational assessment and how to use them in an effective balance.

THE CHAPTER WILL HELP YOU TO:

○ Understand the wide scope of vocational assessment

○ Appreciate the characteristics of the particular vocational qualifications you are assessing

○ Understand the types and sources of evidence.

KEY POINTS

1. Different vocational qualifications emphasise different balances of evidence - some qualifications are practically based with small amounts of knowledge to be assessed, while others need larger and wider areas of knowledge.

2. The characteristics of a vocational qualification will indicate the sources and amount of evidence candidates need to collect, and the assessors to assess.

3. The wide range of possible sources of evidence gives candidates opportunities to present evidence of their competence according to their own preferences and circumstances.

The basis of assessment

Different qualifications, awarding bodies and standards emphasise differing balances between performance and knowledge evidence. Assessors need to be aware of the basis of vocational assessment so they can effectively advise their candidates on the best forms of evidence collection.

> Different qualifications have differing balances between sources of evidence.

National standards define what candidates should do and what they should know to be qualified as competent.

Candidates collect evidence of their competence to present to an assessor who judges this evidence against the requirements of the standards.

The basis is similar to the legal model where evidence is used to build a convincing case. The candidate collects, structures and presents evidence to convince the assessor that he or she is competent.

Types of evidence

There are two types of evidence:

1. Evidence that shows what a candidate can do.

> Examples of evidence are presented in Chapter 5.

This is known as performance, or primary evidence.

2. Evidence that shows what a candidate knows or understands.

This is known as supplementary, supporting or knowledge evidence.

To demonstrate competence, candidates must collect both types of evidence.

The diagram opposite shows the two types of evidence and their sources.

Assessment by the presentation of evidence

EVIDENCE is of two types

PERFORMANCE EVIDENCE	SUPPLEMENTARY EVIDENCE
Shows that a candidate	Shows that a candidate
CAN DO	KNOWS AND UNDERSTANDS

The two types of evidence are defined within the standards by performance criteria, range statements and guidance on evidence collection.

Sources of evidence

Observation of performance

In work situations, set tasks in a work environment, simulations or training exercises and assignments.

Primarily gives performance evidence.

Questioning

Verbal, while performing activities or at a review meeting

Written, such as multiple-choice, essays and projects

Primarily gives supplementary evidence.

Reports

Brief reflective reports by candidates on their experience, activities and role

Work diaries, procedural notes, assignments and projects

Gives both performance and supplementary evidence.

Testimonies

Managers, colleagues and clients giving evidence about the candidate's performance and/or knowledge. This evidence can be collected verbally or in writing.

Gives both performance and supplementary evidence.

Products

Items that are produced as a result of performance, for example, letters/memos, computer printouts, completed documents and finished products (such as brickwork, hairstyle or food).

Primarily gives performance evidence.

The two types of evidence can be collected from a wide range of sources to suit the needs and preferences of candidates, assessors and organisations.

National standards are available across most employment sectors and at levels 1 to 5, where 1 refers to simple and routine activities carried out under supervision and 5 refers to more complex activities carried out with autonomy and initiative. These standards have different amounts of detail and different emphases on performance and knowledge. This means that there will be different emphases on the sources of evidence required for qualifications.

> NVQs are awarded at levels from 1 to 5 (see Chapter 4).
>
> GNVQs are presently awarded at foundation, intermediate and advanced levels.

For example, a level 1 administration NVQ concentrates on the performance of routine tasks such as filing and mail handling. The main source of evidence collection is therefore by observation of performance, probably with simple questioning to cover the knowledge specified in the standards.

In a level 4 training NVQ the knowledge specification is much wider and deeper, requiring the appreciation of concepts and theories. In this qualification, knowledge needs to be assessed across a wider scope and therefore the sources of evidence may tend towards questioning, essays, assignments and reports which will support performance.

GNVQs provide a base of vocational skills and knowledge to equip candidates for employment, further training or higher education. Sources of evidence will tend to be projects, work experience, enterprise activities and written tests.

> Think about the balance between performance and knowledge for the activities in the qualification you are assessing.

TO DO !

Look at the qualifications you will be assessing. What is the emphasis and balance of the evidence? Is it:

(a) Practically based, emphasising observation of performance supported by simple questioning and brief reports and/or diaries?

OR

(b) A variety of evidence concerning more complex activities with large amounts of knowledge to assess? Sources of evidence would be based on evidence of performance with support from knowledge evidence gained from questioning, assignments, reflective reports and storyboards.

OR, somewhere between these two?

What sources of evidence do you think will be most realistic and effective for the qualifications you will be assessing?

Balance of evidence

Assessors need to be aware of the requirements and characteristics of the qualifications they are assessing so that they can advise and judge candidates on the most effective basis.

Here are some examples of how qualifications, awarding bodies and standards influence the balance of evidence collection.

This first case study illustrates the approach to assessing a practically-based NVQ in a college setting.

➡ CASE STUDY

Annette is a lecturer in a college of further education taking trainees through an NVQ level 1 in carpentry and joinery. The standards are very practically based and trainees are assessed by completing set tasks after a period of instruction.

Annette negotiates assessments with trainees and records these on an action plan which gives details of training and assessments completed and planned. At assessments, Annette observes trainees' performance during set tasks and uses a checklist to ensure they perform to the standard required for the NVQ. Understanding and knowledge are tested by trainees completing a job knowledge/practical workbook which has exercises and questions covering the standards. By using both methods, all aspects of the standards are covered.

As an assessor, Annette uses the material produced within the college and applies her own vocational experience to assessing performance by observing the trainees in class and set tasks.

The second case study describes a different approach in assessing management NVQs. The difference lies in the manager's previous experience and the knowledge requirements of the standards.

➡ CASE STUDY

Ravi is an assessor for a level 4 management NVQ. Candidates start with a development interview which introduces the standards and gives time for self-assessment and development planning. Most candidates find they need some training and development in aspects of the standards and this is arranged with a local provider. Candidates often have experience which means that they are ready for assessment. Ravi discusses with each candidate how they can collect evidence of this competence. This evidence consists of products from the workplace supported by reflective reports and testimonies. To cover specific knowledge requirements in the standards, candidates may write an essay or complete a work-based assignment. The level 4 management NVQ covers a wide range of principles and methods such as effective communication, resource planning and control, job analysis and forecasting techniques.

The assessors in these case studies will require similar skills and knowledge, but they need the ability to adapt these to the requirements of the qualification and candidates.

The following case study describes an approach to assessing business GNVQs.

➡ CASE STUDY

Chris is a teacher in a school offering the business GNVQs. Assessment is seen as an integral part of learning during the GNVQ programme. The students generally agree with Chris the elements, performance criteria and range to be addressed. Together they agree activities which cover the performance criteria and range. They consider ways that the core skills and grading will be addressed. These discussions form the basis of an assessment plan. They check the assessment plan against the evidence indicators in the standards.

The school intends to build a bank of activities to draw upon in the future, but as yet, in the early days, much of the work is pioneering.

It is important to use the rest of this workbook applying its principles and material to your own situation and the qualifications you are assessing.

4. EXPLAINING NATIONAL STANDARDS AND ASSESSMENT

THIS CHAPTER IS ABOUT:

○ National standards, NVQs and GNVQs

○ The structure of national standards

○ Characteristics of vocational qualifications

○ The roles in the assessment process

○ How candidates go through the assessment process.

TDLB STANDARDS

Although not directly related to performance criteria in D32 or D33, this section is necessary to enable assessors to help candidates relate standards to their work and thereby identify evidence.

THE CHAPTER WILL HELP YOU TO:

○ Understand the background, characteristics and structure of national standards, NVQs and GNVQs

○ Explain the qualifications and assessment process to candidates

○ Be clear about your place in the assessment team and how candidates will go through the assessment process.

KEY POINTS

1. Vocational qualifications are part of a national initiative to increase the skill levels in the workforce.

2. National standards include units and elements of competence.

3. NVQs and GNVQs have important characteristics of benefit to employers and candidates.

4. Assessors are part of an assessment team made up of candidates, assessors, verifiers, trainers and managers.

5. Candidates register for a qualification and are then helped by assessors to plan their way through the assessment process.

One of the first things an assessor needs to do is to make sure that candidates know the layout and content of national standards and how they are going to be assessed.

What are national standards?

National standards for NVQs are being developed by lead bodies for their own employment sector. The standards describe what is expected by that sector for the competent performance of work.

This development is part of a national training initiative supported by government, employers and educationalists which sets out to prepare people for work, raise the competence of the workforce and provide a new way of qualifying people to do their jobs.

A national initiative to prepare people for work, develop standards of competence and vocational qualifications.

This initiative is supported by government, employers and educationalists.

This national initiative is:

O   Preparing people for work through GNVQs and NVQs

O   Setting standards

O   Assessing people against national standards

O   Establishing a national framework of standards and qualifications.

There are agreed targets to develop lifetime learning involving the use of national standards and the attainment of vocational qualifications.

What are National Vocational Qualifications (NVQs)?

The National Vocational Qualifications (NVQs) available under this initiative are awarded to those who have been assessed, according to national standards, as competently performing work activities. Assessment takes place over a period of time and will be related to employment needs.

NVQs and GNVQs are all part of a national initiative to prepare people for work and increase the skill levels of the workforce.

What are General National Vocational Qualifications (GNVQs)?

General National Vocational Qualifications (GNVQs) provide a broad-based vocational education for young people and adults. They are designed to be used in schools and colleges. They concentrate on key areas of knowledge including core skills related to a vocational area. Assessment takes place over a period of time and will be related to the needs of the workplace.

The structure of NVQs and GNVQs

Each NVQ and GNVQ has a unique title including the level of the qualification.

An NVQ or a GNVQ is a statement of competence, incorporating national standards, which covers a particular area of work at a specific level of achievement. The qualification has a unique title reflecting the area of work and the level (e.g. health care: operating department practice NVQ level 3). All NVQs have a qualification level from 1 to 5 dependent on the complexity, scope and responsibility of the activities described in the units of the NVQ. GNVQs are currently available at foundation, intermediate and advanced levels to aid progression in skills and knowledge.

NVQs and GNVQs are made up of units of competence expressed in elements.

An NVQ and GNVQ is subdivided into units of competence, each reflecting an area of activity (e.g. 'data processing' is an NVQ unit and 'business systems' is a GNVQ unit). A unit is the smallest part of the competence statement for which a certificate can be awarded (unit certification). A number of units together make up the award of a full NVQ or GNVQ certificate.

Each element has performance criteria and range.

A unit consists of elements of competence with their related performance criteria and range.

The performance criteria describe the standards for competent performance.

The range specifies the breadth of competence which may include the contexts and situations where performance must be demonstrated, as well as equipment, procedures and environments.

Assessors use the performance criteria and range to judge a candidate's competence.

The structure of each unit of an NVQ and GNVQ is as follows:

UNIT TITLE which describes the area of work to be accredited.

ELEMENTs which describe the activities required in this area of work.

PERFORMANCE CRITERIA for the elements, which if met consistently will show that the activity in the element is being carried out to the required standard.

RANGEs for the elements, which define in more detail the breadth of applications in which a candidate would be required to be competent.

UNIT TITLE
ELEMENT TITLE
PERFORMANCE CRITERIA
RANGE

Important characteristics of NVQs

NVQs identify the skills and knowledge people need at work to do their job competently to national standards. Individuals can be assessed and qualified in their normal place of work related to performance in their job. Training and development can be directly linked to work needs and performance.

Attractive to employers and candidates.

NVQs are:

O **Based on national standards.**

These standards have been developed by employers themselves and are relevant to the needs of employment. National standards mean that qualifications are portable between companies and across the country.

Based on national standards giving transferable qualifications.

O **Qualifications related to what people do in an occupational area.**

NVQs give credit for what people do in work. This makes the qualifications real and relevant to employers and employees.

O **Assessed in the workplace.**

NVQs are based on work activities and assessed in the workplace making them relevant to work.

The spectre of exams and tests disappears as candidates are assessed in their normal work environment. Evidence of competent performance can be gathered by a variety of methods overcoming the exam or test-based emphasis on qualifications. This also enables employers to apply the qualification to their own particular work needs.

O **Qualifications which have no pre-entry qualification rules.**

Candidates can register for the qualification which fits the job they do without the need for previous exams or training. NVQs are structured to provide a ladder of progression according to the job responsibilities of people.

There are no entry requirements or time limitations for the qualifications.

O **Not tied to any training course or programme.**

NVQs are concerned with assessing people as competent at work. How they achieve that competence is not a factor of the qualification structure. Candidates can become competent through a mixture of work experience, company training or traditional courses. Employers have a greater choice of how they develop their workforce and are not confined to traditional methods.

The qualifications do not specify any particular programme of training. Employers and candidates can negotiate the best ways to develop competence.

Important characteristics of GNVQs

GNVQs are about work but are studied at school or college. They allow tutors and students to devise individual learning programmes.

GNVQs:

○ **are based on national standards.**

These standards offer preparation for the world of work.

| GNVQs give a wide experience of an occupation preparing young people for the world of work. |

○ **are qualifications related to a broad occupational area.**

The qualifications provide broad experience in an occupational area giving access to wider job opportunities and transferable skills.

| GNVQs can be taken with other qualifications to provide a broader experience. |

○ **can be taken with A or AS levels or NVQ units.**

GNVQs can be integrated into a variety of programmes taking account of students' preferences, needs and aspirations.

Who is involved?

Assessors and internal verifiers

Assessors and internal verifiers are appointed by an approved centre. They should be trained and qualified to work in an approved centre to assess candidates' performance and knowledge as specified in the national standards. They will support the candidates in planning their route through the qualifications and assess evidence presented by candidates. Assessors and internal verifiers will also be responsible for operating the appeals and equal opportunities procedures required of an approved centre, ensuring equality of access to qualifications for candidates. Assessors and internal verifiers will need to know the structure and content of the standards and how to use the competence statements to make judgments about candidates' performance.

> Assessors and internal verifiers play the key assessment and quality roles in the assessment process. For more detail on these and other roles in the assessment team, see Chapter 2.

Candidates

These are individuals who want to gain a vocational qualification. They will be assessed in the normal course of their job or arrange for assessment through a college, assessment centre or training provider if they are not employed. NVQs and GNVQs have a policy of open access which means that anyone can apply to do the qualification whatever their age or previous qualifications.

> Candidates are those wanting to gain a vocational qualification.

They will need the support of assessors to plan their way through the qualification and to gather evidence of their competence. Candidates will have to register at a centre approved to offer assessment for the qualification they decide to take, and this decision will be influenced by their vocational plans. They will need to know the structure and content of the standards and how they will be assessed by assessors using the guidance in the standards.

Candidates may need the support of trainers to develop their competence in some areas of the standards.

Trainers, teachers and lecturers

Trainers, teachers and lecturers will be involved in developing the competence of candidates. To do this they can use the structure of the qualifications and the performance criteria to design programmes and learning objectives. The assessment of vocational qualifications is independent of any training programme, and provision of training is a local decision based on the needs of the candidates and their organisations.

> Trainers, teachers and lecturers may be involved in developing the competence of candidates.

Developing the competence of individuals to national standards allows trainers, teachers and lecturers to use a wider range of training methods to suit individual learning styles and organisational resources. Courses, assignments, projects, workshops, self-study and distance learning are all useful methods to develop competence.

Managers

Managers can release resources and use competences and NVQs to achieve business objectives.

National standards offer managers a definition of competent performance in the workplace. Managers can use the structure and content of national standards to:

O Define job and departmental responsibilities

O Recruit, train and motivate the workforce

O Define and present statements of quality performance.

Managers will need to understand the structure and assessment of the qualifications so they can make informed decisions about planning and resourcing the implementation of NVQs. Managers have a responsibility to ensure the appeals and equal opportunities procedures are being applied effectively and that resources are allocated to the effective implementation of the qualifications.

The following exercise identifies all those who contribute to the assessment process in your organisation:

✱ EXERCISE

Who is involved in the assessment team of your organisation?

List the people and their titles or roles if you know them.

How do they contribute to the assessment process?

How do candidates achieve a vocational qualification?

For NVQs, candidates do not have to start at level 1: the decision as to which level they go for will be based on their present work and previous experience. For GNVQs, candidates will normally progress from foundation, through intermediate to advanced. To follow a vocational qualification, candidates must register with a centre approved by an awarding body to assess for the qualification. This may be a work organisation, college or school.

The awarding body sets and applies the criteria for a centre to be approved. These criteria include:

O Having adequate staff, management support and physical and financial resources

O Developing competent assessors and internal verifiers

O Checking arrangements for the process of assessment and verification

O Implementing appeals and equal opportunity procedures.

> Awarding body criteria to be an approved centre to offer a vocational qualification.

Once registered, the candidates begin planning their routes through to the qualification with assessors.

This plan will involve candidates in:

O Looking at previous experience

The assessor will discuss what candidates have done in the past both in their present job and other experiences. Assessors will take account of any relevant experience and this will mean that candidates will not be trained in what they can already do. This process is known as the accreditation of prior learning (APL).

> The candidate's route through the assessment process.
>
> See Chapters 11 and 12 for worked examples of this process, including examples of documents used in the process.

O Planning how the units will be assessed

O Identifying any training required

O Arranging assessments.

✻ EXERCISE

Explain how candidates go through the assessment process in your centre. Make a note of any forms that are used for self-assessment, planning and reviewing. Include copies in your portfolio.

Candidates are encouraged to identify and present evidence of their competence over a period of time.

See Chapters 3 and 5 for more detail on the sources of evidence.

This evidence can come from the range of sources described in Chapter 3:

○ Observation of performance

○ Reports

○ Testimonies

○ Products

○ Questioning.

NVQs assessed mainly in the workplace.

Most NVQ assessments will take place in a work environment and, when sufficient evidence is presented, an assessor will be able to accredit the candidate as being competent, according to the national standards.

Assessors of GNVQs will assess in a range of environments.

GNVQs will be assessed by a variety of methods, mostly within a learning and training programme.

Judging evidence is covered in Chapter 6.

The standards frequently offer guidance for each element on the amount and type of evidence a candidate needs to present to be assessed as competent.

A full NVQ or GNVQ certificate is awarded when all the units are complete at a particular level, although individual units can be certificated separately (unit certification).

TO DO !

Look at examples of NVQs or GNVQs that you use.

On a copy of an element from these standards identify: the performance criteria, unit and element titles, range and the assessment guidance or evidence indicators, if present.

On the back of this copy describe how you would explain to a candidate what each of these terms mean. Keep a copy of this in your portfolio.

Check your explanations with the definitions in Chapter 13 'Language and terms'.

5. IDENTIFYING AND RECOGNISING EVIDENCE

THIS CHAPTER IS ABOUT:

○ The knowledge that assessors need in order to explain to their candidates how to identify evidence

○ Types, sources and examples of evidence

○ The first step in the assessment process.

TDLB STANDARDS

Elements D321 and D331 require a knowledge of types and sources of evidence covered in this chapter. Knowledge of evidence allows the assessor to make assessment plans with candidates.

THIS CHAPTER WILL HELP YOU TO:

○ Relate national standards to your candidates' experiences

○ Explain examples of evidence to your candidates

○ Make assessment plans with your candidates.

KEY POINTS

1. When taking candidates through the assessment process, the first step is to help candidates relate the standards to their experiences.

2. Candidates need to identify the evidence that will show their assessors they are competent.

3. Assessors and candidates agree these evidence requirements on an assessment plan.

Evidence as the basis of assessment

Candidates are assessed as competent when, according to the national standards, there is sufficient evidence of their competence.

Assessors need to know about:

○ types of evidence

○ sources of evidence

○ how to make judgements about evidence.

Types and sources of evidence were covered briefly in Chapter 3 but these topics are covered in more detail, with examples, in this chapter. The criteria used to judge evidence are covered in Chapter 6.

> The main examples rely on an element from an NVQ and are therefore related to the workplace. A GNVQ example is presented towards the end of the chapter.

The main example in this chapter relates to an element in an NVQ and therefore concentrates on workplace evidence. At the end of the chapter is an element from an advanced GNVQ with comments on evidence requirements.

On the next page is an element from the national standards for business administration which will be used to provide illustrations for the points about evidence covered in this chapter.

Two types of evidence were presented in Chapter 3:

1. Performance or primary evidence

2. Supplementary, supporting or knowledge evidence.

1. Performance evidence

> Performance evidence demonstrates to an assessor that a candidate performs the activities described in the performance criteria.

NVQs concentrate on the performance of work activities and performance evidence is most important. Performance criteria in the standards describe what assessors should observe to accredit candidates as competent. Documents or products that occur as a result of performance are also performance evidence. Performance evidence can come from simulation of work activities as a set task or on a training course (such as in-tray exercises, role play and demonstrations).

> Chapter 7 covers the skills of gathering performance evidence by observing candidates.

> GNVQs do not rely on observed performance in a work situation as NVQs do. Assessment will generally be based on projects and work experience.

GNVQs tend to be assessed by projects, work experience and other activities such as simulation and presentations.

For the following NVQ administration standard, element L1.5.1 'Process incoming and outgoing telecommunications', performance evidence would be collected by observing candidates in their normal place of work processing telephone calls, faxes and messages.

ADMINISTRATION STANDARDS

UNIT L1.5 PROCESS INFORMATION

ELEMENT 1.5.1 Process incoming and outgoing telecommunications

PERFORMANCE CRITERIA

A. Communications are responded to promptly and clearly using approved organisation manner

B. Callers are correctly identified and requirements established accurately

C. Queries are answered within own area of authority or referred to the appropriate person

D. Outgoing calls, for self or on behalf of others, are correctly obtained

E. Relevant information is courteously obtained and checked

F. Relevant information is communicated promptly and accurately to the appropriate person

G. Faults are promptly reported to the appropriate person

H. Recording of communications, when required, is in accordance with organisational procedures

RANGE STATEMENTS

Communications: internal: external

Telecommunications: voice: data: text

KNOWLEDGE / UNDERSTANDING

: types and use of telecommunication equipment

: effective and efficient communication

:establishing rapport and goodwill with callers

:composition of messages

: listening, interpreting, extracting and recording information

: structure, product and services of organisation

: communication styles used by organisation

: confirmation procedures

: policy and procedures on security, safety and emergencies

: recording / reporting procedures

This element, taken from the administration lead body standards, is used to provide examples illustrating types, sources and judgements of evidence.

Check back to Chapter 4 for an explanation of the structure of standards.

In Chapter 4 the range was described as details of the applications in which a candidate would be required to be competent. In these administration standards the range is referred to as 'Range statements'.

These administration standards include a specification of the knowledge and understanding required to support competent performance. Assessors will use this specification to check candidate's understanding.

You would need to see the candidate over a number of days to ensure consistent performance and to check that all the performance criteria are fulfilled across the range. This is why assessors are best selected from people alongside candidates in a supervisory role.

2. Supplementary, supporting or knowledge evidence

Supplementary evidence shows a candidate's knowledge and understanding. Competent performance must be supported by an understanding of why things are done in a certain way and what action may be necessary if things go wrong.

As well as performance evidence, elements usually require supplementary (sometimes referred to as supporting) evidence of underpinning knowledge and understanding. This evidence may be necessary to ensure that a candidate is performing work activities with understanding or to cover contingencies and other situations defined in the range.

In most cases, by observing a performance, you can infer that a candidate knows certain things. Using the administration standards example, if you observed a candidate answering a number of phone queries on an outside line, you could infer that the first three performance criteria had been fulfilled. However you may want to check on a candidate's knowledge of organisation procedures and who are appropriate persons for different queries. You may not be able reasonably to infer that a candidate knows these procedures purely from a series of observations of performance.

You can check a candidate's knowledge in a number of ways.

Chapter 8 covers the skill of questioning candidates and others.

The first is by asking questions. This is easy and natural to do verbally during or after the observation or at a specific interview when you discuss how the candidate got on.

Written questions are suitable. For example:

'To whom would you refer the following incoming queries?'

a) a complaint about service

b) a query about an invoice

c) a request for product information

For a full range of sources of supplementary evidence see the following section, 'Sources of evidence'.

Other methods to check knowledge could include asking candidates to keep a work diary or write reflective reports or notes about what they have done. Assessment methods are not usually prescribed by awarding bodies. Assessors can decide on methods which best suit their candidates, the standards and their organisation. It is important to select those methods which will ensure full coverage of the requirements in the standards.

As explained in Chapter 3, some of the knowledge specified to support standards is complex and broad, for example in the management standards published by the Management Charter Initiative (MCI). It would be difficult to cover all the knowledge requirements by verbal questioning, and some additional evidence is required by other methods such as assignments and case studies which specifically target the knowledge to be assessed.

Knowledge evidence supports the observation of performance and should assure an assessor of the candidate's competence.

Sources of evidence

Evidence of a candidate's competence is available from a number of sources which were introduced in Chapter 3.

Performance evidence can be gathered from:

O Candidate's performance

O Products arising out of the performance, for example a sales display or cooked item

O Documents arising in the normal course of work, for example memos, forms and reports

O Skills tests or tasks in a simulated situation, course work and assessments from training

O Projects, assignments or case studies

O Testimonies from colleagues, previous employers or work experience providers.

> Sources of evidence showing what a candidate can do.

Supplementary, supporting evidence can be gathered from:

O Oral questions

O Written tests (such as short-answer questions, multiple-choice questions and essays)

O Reflective reports, projects and diaries.

> Sources of evidence showing a candidate has knowledge and understanding.

In the administration standards example the following are possible sources of evidence that may occur in the workplace.

Candidates and assessors need to identify and agree what evidence can be gathered from available sources to show a candidate's competence.

> **Sources of evidence for the example element from the administration lead body standards.**

O Observation of candidate using the telephone and fax in the normal place of work

O Verbal and/or written questions on procedures and policy to cover all aspects of the range and performance criteria

O Memos, checklists and reports generated by the candidate in the course of work

O Reports and testimonies from supervisors

O Fault-reporting diary kept by candidate

O Testimonial letters from clients

O Attendance on a training course for telephone manner, for example. Evidence could come from exercises conducted on the course and recorded on an assessment sheet, cassette or video.

> **Sources and type of evidence are agreed with candidates and recorded on an assessment plan.**

Assessors will agree the evidence with candidates for particular elements and record this on an assessment plan. (See the worked example for NVQs in Chapter 11 and for GNVQs in Chapter 12; there are examples of documents in those chapters.)

This makes it clear to the assessor and candidate just what is expected in the way of evidence and therefore how the candidate will be able to show competence.

Some assessment systems have previously agreed assessment plans which give assessors and candidates the structure for evidence identification and collection. The case study below gives an example of this.

➡ CASE STUDY

Arnold is an assessor for construction NVQs at a college of further education. He had an apprenticeship in a trade and ran his own jobbing builder firm. He joined the college and gained further trade and teaching qualifications.

Trainees following construction NVQs work through a workbook produced by the lead body for construction. This workbook contains practical tasks and job knowledge checks. The workbook is used as a guide for assessors and candidates in what they should do and know. Assessments are arranged when candidates have received training and are sufficiently practised to be ready. The workbook is used as an assessment checklist and question paper, giving the assessor a format on which to base decisions. Arnold records his assessment decision in the workbook.

Evidence for GNVQ assessment is founded on projects and assignments, documented work experience and evidence of understanding underpinning knowledge. In the following GNVQ advanced business element the evidence indicators provide suggestions of the type of activities required of candidates in order to demonstrate that the performance criteria and range have been satisfied. The sources of evidence would be projects, one of which should focus on a particular organisation's communication system. Work placements would provide experience of the organisation's communication systems. Learning opportunities could concentrate on the structure, running and effectiveness of communication systems. The unit test assesses the underpinning knowledge of the unit.

> An example from an advanced GNVQ to illustrate evidence for assessment of these qualifications.

GNVQ ADVANCED BUSINESS

UNIT 2 BUSINESS SYSTEMS

ELEMENT 2.2 Investigate communication systems

PERFORMANCE CRITERIA

1. Purposes of communication systems used by business organisations are explained.

2. A business organisation's communication systems are investigated and described.

3. Effectiveness of systems in supporting the functions of the business organisation is evaluated.

4. Users' opinions of investigated communication systems are described.

5. Electronic technology changing communication systems is identified.

RANGE

Purposes: internal, external; handling information, taking decisions, informing actions

Communication systems: internal, external; face to face; correspondence; telecommunications; computer-aided

Electronic technology: network computer systems, electronic mail, enhanced telephone systems

Evaluation criteria: accuracy, cost-effectiveness, security

EVIDENCE INDICATORS

Examples of communication systems within a business organisation indicating how new technology is changing communication systems and an evaluation of accuracy, efficiency, cost-effectiveness and security of systems. Evidence should demonstrate understanding of the implications of the range dimensions in relation to the element. The unit test will confirm the candidate's coverage of range.

---

6. JUDGING EVIDENCE

THIS CHAPTER IS ABOUT:

- ○ The criteria for judging evidence
- ○ Valid evidence
- ○ Authentic evidence
- ○ Current evidence
- ○ Sufficient evidence.

TDLB STANDARDS

This chapter, about judging evidence, is at the root of elements D322, D323, D324, D332 and D333.

The exercises in the chapter will provide good practice for your learning and evidence for your portfolio.

THE CHAPTER WILL HELP YOU TO:

- ○ Make decisions about evidence presented to you by a candidate
- ○ Judge whether or not candidates are competent
- ○ Explain to candidates when and how to collect more evidence.

KEY POINTS

1. Candidates must present valid, authentic, current and sufficient evidence to convince assessors they are competent.

2. Choosing what evidence to collect is governed by these criteria.

3. Not all evidence has the same importance and weight.

4. There are exercises to illustrate some of the issues to consider when judging evidence.

It is the assessor's job to judge the evidence presented by a candidate.

To make this judgement the assessor must apply the criteria represented in the mnemonic VACS.

The assessor must ask:

Is the evidence presented by the candidate

V - VALID?

A - AUTHENTIC?

The criteria used to judge evidence.

C - CURRENT?

S - SUFFICIENT?

Valid evidence

Valid evidence tells you about how a candidate can perform and relates to the performance criteria and range being assessed. This is why, for example, observing performance in the workplace provides valid evidence for NVQs.

VALID EVIDENCE

What does this evidence tell me about how the candidate performs activities, according to the national standards?

Attendance on a training course does not guarantee that a candidate has acquired any skills. Signed assessments from a training course of a candidate's performance on clearly described tasks that are matched to the performance criteria in the qualification should provide valid evidence of competence. For NVQs the training environment provides a simulated workplace and therefore further evidence will probably need to be sought from the workplace.

So it can be seen that not all evidence has the same importance or value when making judgements about a candidate's competence.

Evidence that a candidate presents to you needs to be relevant to the qualification concerned. It is important to impress on candidates the need to select evidence that relates to the performance criteria and range in the elements. Sometimes an item of evidence may be relevant to a number of elements.

Documents used by candidates do not necessarily tell you that they can do the task or that they understand what they are doing. A candidate's work diary or log could offer a lot of valuable information about their performance, whereas a procedural checklist gives little valid information about a candidate's competence.

Similarly, certificates tell you that a candidate has followed a course of study and passed an exam or assessment at the end. Certificates don't often tell you about the candidate's actual performance in a workplace or what criteria were used for the assessment.

Written references which tell you about the attributes of a person rarely provide valid evidence relevant to the standards. Details of how considerate or honest a person is tells you little about how they perform activities using the criteria of assessment in NVQs or GNVQs.

It is important to bear in mind, at all times, the question:

What does this evidence tell me about the candidate's performance of activities, according to the national standards?

The answer to this question will tell you the value you can place on evidence. In assessment for NVQs, frequently the most valuable and valid form of evidence is seeing a candidate working in the workplace.

Authentic evidence

The issue here concerns the question:

Can you be sure that the evidence tells you about the individual performance of the candidate?

As an assessor you need to be confident that the evidence presented is an accurate and true reflection of the candidate's own activities and competence.

Group work, projects completed away from the assessor, company-produced checklists or policies, team training assessments or documents about the candidate must all be treated with healthy scepticism. This is not to say that candidates will lie or falsify evidence. Some evidence that candidates present may not be individual or specific enough for you to be sure that the candidate is competent.

> AUTHENTIC EVIDENCE
>
> Can you be sure that the evidence tells you something about the individual performance of the candidate?

Current evidence

The issue here concerns the question:

Does this evidence demonstrate the current competence of the candidate?

Is the candidate's evidence demonstrating competence which is still current practice, for example with regard to legislation? This is a particularly important question when considering evidence from a previous number of years. Assessors need to check whether the equipment, work practices and regulations have changed since the evidence was collected.

As an assessor you will also need to feel confident that the candidate has retained the competence which was demonstrated in the past, to the present day.

> **CURRENT EVIDENCE**
>
> Does the evidence demonstrate what the candidate can do now?

Sufficient evidence

The issue here concerns the question:

Does the evidence cover all the performance criteria and the range adequately, taking full account of the assessment guidance?

There is a tendency to believe that quantity is quality. This is not so.

> **SUFFICIENT EVIDENCE**
>
> Does the evidence cover all the performance criteria and the range, taking full account of the assessment guidance?

The amount of evidence required to demonstrate competence is prescribed by the standards being assessed. The assessment requirements will always be:

O   All the performance criteria must be covered by the evidence

O   All aspects of the range must be covered by the evidence.

In addition to these two basic criteria, there may be additional assessment requirements in the assessment guidance with regard to knowledge specifications or recommendations on type and amount of evidence.

Assessors will need to be sure that there is enough evidence, on a repeated basis, to cover all aspects of the standards without unnecessary repetition.

Assessors should be confident that all the performance criteria, range and underpinning knowledge are covered by enough evidence of the right quality.

TDLB STANDARDS

This exercise gives you the opportunity to practise judging evidence. This covers performance criteria in elements D322, D323, D324, D332 and D333.

Keep a copy of this exercise in your portfolio.

* EXERCISE

Below are three examples of evidence an assessor may receive for Element L1.5.1 from the administration standards referred to in Chapter 5.

For each example make notes on the validity, authenticity, currency and sufficiency of the evidence offered and then discuss your notes with a colleague.

There is an analysis following the examples.

EXAMPLE 1

Talat explains that he has recently attended the company training course on telephone manner. As evidence he presents the attendance certificate, course programme and notes and tell you about an assessment exercise undertaken in pairs.

EXAMPLE 2

Sheila produces the company policy on customer treatment and a checklist of how to answer telephone calls. She explains that her performance is a matter for regular scrutiny by her supervisor and suggests you talk to her.

EXAMPLE 3

Liam shows you a portfolio which contains

● A summary of experience, which states he has worked in the organisation for 2 years as a clerical officer, and that previously he had been involved with taking and making, by telephone and fax, reservations for a large hotel in the centre of Birmingham

● A witness testimony from his supervisor, which lists the performance criteria and range and has brief descriptions of how the performance criteria and range were demonstrated over the last 6 months

● A fault log book which he has used recently to report and monitor faults.

The candidate suggests you may need to observe his performance at work to check the coverage of performance criteria and range.

Analysis of evidence examples from exercise

EXAMPLE 1

VALID?

Does the evidence match the standards? The evidence offered by Talat does not. There is no evidence that clearly covers any of the performance criteria or range. Attending a training course does not demonstrate that he can perform work activities. Although the assessment exercise sounds as if it was practical, there appears to be no documentary evidence of the criteria used for assessment and therefore what and how well Talat performed.

AUTHENTIC?

What evidence can be attributed to the candidate? The assessor can ask questions on how the programme and exercise relate to the performance criteria, range and Talat's job. The assessment exercise does not appear to provide evidence of his individual performance in work situations.

CURRENT?

Does the evidence show current competence? The description does not provide information on current performance in the workplace or, indeed, how long ago the course took place.

SUFFICIENT?

There is not sufficient evidence to say that Talat is competent. The example concentrates on one item or aspect of evidence. The assessor and candidate must agree on how other evidence will support competence and cover all aspects of the element. Other evidence could include: workplace observations, memos or messages that Talat completes, a work log describing his performance, targeted questioning of his supervisor to check his performance against the performance criteria in the element, or a reflective report from Talat on what is important in answering the telephone.

OVERALL?

This evidence provides little to help make a judgement about Talat's competence. This is not to say that his training experience tells you nothing about him. Experience of such a training course indicates that learning has had a chance. This should mean that Talat is ready for work-based assessment immediately. An assessor should make arrangements with the candidate to observe his performance at work and generate the performance evidence from this observation.

EXAMPLE 2

VALID?

The actual evidence offered is of little value. The company-produced policy and checklist say nothing about whether Sheila performs to the standards. The suggestion of talking to her supervisor would provide supporting evidence of value and ideally the supervisor would need to relate her judgements to the standards.

AUTHENTIC?

Production of company documents says nothing about an individual's performance. An interview with Sheila's supervisor could ensure authentic and reliable evidence about her individual performance.

CURRENT?

The suggested evidence appears to be current. A company checklist would probably cover most of the performance criteria - but this needs to be checked. Evidence from Sheila's supervisor would ensure current performance.

SUFFICIENT?

There is not sufficient evidence so far to say that Sheila is competent. The example concentrates on one aspect of the evidence required. The assessor and candidate must agree on how other evidence will support competence and cover all aspects of the element. Other evidence could include: workplace observations, memos or messages Sheila takes, a work log describing her performance, targeted questioning of her supervisor to check her performance against the performance criteria in the element, or a reflective report from Sheila on what is important in processing incoming and outgoing telecommunications.

OVERALL?

The most useful suggestion here is talking to Sheila's supervisor. There is regular monitoring of the candidate's performance and, if that is based on the company policy and checklist, an assessor has a base to begin discussions relating company documentation to the national standards. It would appear that the assessor could arrange assessments in the workplace. The assessor should plan to make an appointment with Sheila's supervisor.

EXAMPLE 3

VALID?

The portfolio looks like it will provide valid evidence. The summary of experience provides an interesting insight into previous and current activities. The witness testimony claims that Liam is competent. The fault log book is good supporting documentary evidence assuming it covers the procedures detailed in performance criterion L1.5.1G.

AUTHENTIC?

The assessor needs to be sure that the portfolio presents an accurate and true reflection of Liam's own activities and competence. This sort of documentary evidence needs careful checking. The credibility of the witnesses should be questioned (How long have they been supervisors? How close is the supervision? Did they witness the candidate's activities at first hand? Do they understand the standards?). The fault log is part of company procedure and is authentic if completed by the candidate.

CURRENT?

The witness testimony of the supervisor and fault log are current evidence.

SUFFICIENT?

There appears to be evidence from a range of sources. It is difficult to say whether or not the evidence is sufficient without more detail of the content of the testimonies and fault log. The assessor needs to make sure that all performance criteria are covered across the range. Some verbal questioning of Liam would almost certainly be necessary, as would accepting his offer to observe his workplace performance.

OVERALL?

The portfolio appears to provide good evidence for the element. To accredit the element an assessor would probably arrange interviews with Liam, his supervisor and those concerned with the reporting of faults to confirm that he is competent.

TDLB STANDARDS

This exercise generates evidence of your ability to identify evidence. The assessment plan and discussion with a colleague provide evidence for elements D321 and D331.

Make notes of your discussion and keep them and the assessment plan in your portfolio.

Having completed Chapters 5 and 6 about identifying and judging evidence, the following two exercises will give you the opportunity to look at the standards that you will be assessing.

These exercises will provide practice for planning assessments with your candidates. They will help you identify likely sources of evidence relevant to your situation and the standards you will be using.

The exercises cover stage 6 - action and assessment plans, in the worked example presented in Chapter 11. Looking at this worked example will help you be clear about assessment plans - what they include and how they are used.

✱ EXERCISE

Take an element from some standards familiar to you. Imagine a fictional or real candidate and produce an assessment plan identifying evidence that they could gather.

Be as detailed as possible, relating the evidence to the candidate's circumstances. The evidence could include: observation of performance, products, testimonies, projects, assignments and questions to ask the candidate.

National standards:

Unit title:

Element number:

Element title:

Evidence a candidate could gather:

✱ EXERCISE

Having completed the fictional assessment plan in the previous exercise, discuss your ideas and how they meet the criteria - valid, authentic, current and sufficient - with a colleague who knows about NVQ or GNVQ assessment.

Make notes on your ideas and this discussion here.

These notes will provide further evidence of your ability to identify and judge evidence.

This exercise provides the structure for your self-report on the issues of judging evidence and can be put in your portfolio, referenced to elements D322, D323, D324, D332 and D333.

7. OBSERVING PERFORMANCE

THIS CHAPTER IS ABOUT:

O The skill of collecting evidence by observing candidate's performance.

TDLB STANDARDS

This chapter covers the skills of gathering performance evidence by observing candidates. This covers elements D322 and D332. The exercises will be useful for your portfolio.

THE CHAPTER WILL HELP YOU TO:

O Observe candidates in a manner which does not intimidate them

O Make your observations relevant to the standards

O Plan your observations with your candidates

O Decide when to use checklists and how to design them.

KEY POINTS

1. Observation of performance is an important form of evidence.

2. Observations must be natural and non-intimidating for candidates.

3. When carrying out observations, only the performance criteria should be used to make judgements about competence.

It is essential that assessors have the observation skills necessary to collect the required evidence and make accurate judgements.

Observations will normally take place in the course of routine work. You and the candidate will be aware of the performance criteria that are being assessed because these should have been discussed and recorded on an assessment/action plan. If you normally work with a candidate, this provides the most natural way of observing performance. Sometimes you may have to arrange a special occasion to observe a candidate during a set task or in a simulation or training environment. In all cases the important things to remember are:

> Collecting evidence by observing candidates in their normal work activities can provide the most valid and authentic form of evidence for NVQs.

1. Keep it natural

Don't stick out like a sore thumb in the workplace. Try and avoid masses of paper and peering over candidates' shoulders. Give the candidates space to get on with their work. In this way you will get a more realistic performance from them. Making a great occasion of assessments will only provide undue pressure on candidates and make them nervous. You may arrange with the candidates to observe their performance over the period of a week or more. In this case, you will be keeping an eye on the candidates throughout their day.

> Keeping observation natural allows candidates to perform to the best of their ability.
>
> They should be familiar with their surroundings and not intimidated by the assessment process.

2. Keep it relevant

While your observation should be natural and routine it must be relevant to the national standards. To focus your observation you will need to have in mind the performance criteria in an element. When you begin assessing this can be difficult because they are often wordy - there are a lot of them. Early on you may need a copy of the performance criteria from the national standards or a checklist. As you become more familiar with the standards you will get to know what to look for.

> Observations should use the performance criteria in the standards.

Spending some time planning with a candidate helps to make the observation natural and relevant. You can discuss the performance criteria and how the candidate expects to achieve them in this particular work setting. This will mean that you are both clear about what is expected. This clarity between you and the candidate is important to avoid misunderstanding and to build a good relationship.

> Assessment and action plans give a structure to the discussion of what evidence will be collected and how this evidence occurs in the workplace.

Discussions before and after observation can clarify specific points to look for in the assessment. This makes for a much more effective assessment than just being alongside the candidate and then trying to remember whether particular activities in the performance criteria were done or not.

TO DO !

Select an element from standards you will be assessing. Make two checklists:

1. A checklist to guide the planning discussion with a candidate, to clarify what is going to happen during the observations.

2. A checklist that can be used to make sure that observations cover all the performance criteria in the standards.

Now use your planning checklist to discuss the assessment you are going to carry out with a candidate.

After carrying out the assessment spend some time discussing with the candidate what you saw. Make notes on the following questions.

Did the atmosphere feel relaxed?

Did the candidate perform as normal?

Did the candidate feel you got in the way?

Make some notes on this discussion and include them and your checklists in your workbook and/or portfolio. The checklists and notes of the discussion will be relevant evidence for elements D322 and D332.

There are examples of checklists overleaf.

Examples of checklists

<table>
<tr><td>

Things to check when planning assessments:

1. The candidate is clear about the evidence required and the time over which assessment takes place.

2. Copies of standards are available.

3. Copies of recording documentation are available.

4. Everybody involved is informed.

</td><td>

Things to check when carrying out observations and after assessment:

1. The candidate was encouraged to perform naturally.

2. Assessor has all necessary documents, i.e. standards, checklists and recording.

3. Assessor's observations were natural and non-intrusive.

4. After observing, the assessor gave feedback to the candidate.

5. The assessor did not lead or guide the candidate.

</td></tr>
</table>

One way of producing a quick observational checklist is to take a copy of the performance criteria and range statements from the actual standards, and make comments and records on that copy.

Note: You may not be able to use checklists like this, but you must be sure that you observe in the correct manner and cover all the important factors. You will find that as your confidence and experience increase you become more 'natural' and less 'mechanical'.

Different awarding bodies, organisations and assessment centres may give different guidance and documentation to record and carry out observations.

Sometimes you may have pro-forma checklists and sometimes you may need to develop your own.

In some circumstances assessment processes have been designed to be far more mechanical and standardised. Assessors may have checklists given to them as part of awarding body documentation or from their organisation.

Competence assessment allows for a variety of approaches, and it is important for assessors to be familiar with the systems within which they work.

There is more information on observational checklists in Chapter 10 'Recording'.

8. QUESTIONING CANDIDATES AND OTHERS

THIS CHAPTER IS ABOUT:

○ Collecting evidence of candidate's knowledge and understanding by a variety of questioning techniques

○ The questioning techniques of verbal and written questions, assignments and multiple-choice tests

○ Evidence from others about the candidate's competence.

TDLB STANDARDS

This chapter covers the skills of gathering knowledge evidence by questioning.

This covers elements D323 and D332. The exercises will provide evidence for your portfolio.

THE CHAPTER WILL HELP YOU TO:

○ Decide which technique to use when collecting knowledge evidence

○ Ask questions which give candidates the opportunity to present evidence of their knowledge and understanding

○ Direct and guide others in giving evidence for candidates

○ Cover all aspects of the standards by giving candidates the chance to present knowledge evidence.

KEY POINTS

1. Asking questions of candidates and others is a major way of collecting knowledge evidence.

2. There is a variety of techniques in questioning, and this means that candidates and assessors can choose which techniques suit them best.

3. Questions must be relevant and open, to allow candidates to demonstrate their knowledge and understanding.

This chapter covers a range of techniques, all of which can be used to collect evidence of a candidate's knowledge and understanding. All are related to questioning.

These techniques cover:

○ Asking candidates verbal questions

asked during performance or at a review or for a specific reason to cover aspects of the standards.

○ Setting candidates written questions

set through multiple-choice papers, projects and assignments.

○ Asking candidates' colleagues and others to give testimony of what candidates can do or know

Colleagues and others can give evidence verbally or by written testimony to cover specific requirements in the standards, for example to cover the range or knowledge specification. Written testimony can also provide evidence of previous experience.

○ Directing candidates in writing reports and diaries

Although not directly answering questions, reports and diaries can provide knowledge evidence. When writing reports and diaries, candidates should be answering questions that they have set themselves from the standards. In other words, reports and diaries should be based on the requirements of the standards.

This chapter covers all aspects of these techniques. The range of techniques provides assessors and candidates with choices about presenting knowledge evidence.

Candidates can choose how they present evidence, based on their preference of writing or speaking.

Assessment of GNVQs and NVQs at level 3 and above requires evidence from assignments, written questions and projects. Assessors will have to ensure that the evidence is relevant and specific to the standards.

Questioning candidates and 'others' provides supplementary evidence. It can show what a candidate knows and understands, and support the demonstration of performance. The 'others' involved in providing this evidence may be colleagues, managers or clients of the candidate. In these circumstances the evidence is called witness testimony.

Candidates must demonstrate knowledge and performance over the variety of situations described in the range statement. This means that you may observe candidates do one activity and question them about other aspects relating to the range statement. Questions to ask can be identified from the national standards, and awarding bodies may provide further guidance.

For example in the standards for care workers there is an element about greeting a client. The range statement covers different clients from children to older people. It may be that you see the candidate perform this element with children. After the observation you could ask the candidate how greeting older people is different. You will probably need to see them perform this activity with the range of clients, but questioning allows assessors to infer a candidate's knowledge.

✷ EXERCISE

In the example above of a candidate greeting a range of clients, what other questions could you ask a candidate to find out if he or she knows how to greet the variety of clients specified in a range from children to older people?

You may ask candidates to explain verbally, or write short answers, about:

Whether they had done this before and in what circumstances.

How they learnt to greet clients and what was important.

How to be sensitive to people's moods and needs.

How their language would be different with different client groups.

Why they did something in a particular way.

Answers to these questions will give you information about the knowledge a candidate has. You will find guidance in the national standards to give you an idea of the areas you need to cover by questioning.

Asking open questions

What sort of answers would you get from the following questions?

'Have you done this before?'

'You do know how to do this don't you?'

These questions can be answered with a 'yes' or 'no'. They are closed questions and they don't tell you much about the candidate's knowledge. They also make the conversation seem very one-sided.

You need to develop the skill of asking 'open' questions. These are questions that cannot be answered with a 'yes' or 'no' but require some explanation, description or opinion giving.

Examples of open questions are:

'When did you do this before?'

'How would you do this?'

Open questions begin with the words: why?, how?, where?, what? and when?

Open questions start with:
Why?
How?
Where?
What?
When?

Look back to the element from the administration standards in Chapter 5.

Write down three open questions that you could ask a candidate to cover the range statement.

Look at elements from the standards you will be assessing and draw up a list of fifteen questions you could ask candidates to check their knowledge and understanding.

Include copies of the elements and questions in your portfolio.

TDLB STANDARDS

This exercise generates evidence of your ability to collect knowledge evidence and can be used in your portfolio for elements D323 and D332.

You will have realised by now that questions need to be relevant. Questions unearth knowledge, but that knowledge must be linked to the requirements of the standards. Ask questions which give you information about performance criteria, range statements and knowledge evidence in the qualification. You should not ask leading questions which suggest answers to the candidate.

Questioning others - known as witness testimony

Evidence of candidates' knowledge gained from those who work with them or supervise them.

Another source of information about the competence of candidates is to question their colleagues, clients and supervisors. Here again the questions must be relevant to performance criteria. It's no good having supervisors or work placement officers tell you that a candidate is a 'good worker'. You need to question them about the candidate's performance in specific performance criteria. It is useful to let the other people have a copy of the elements from the standards to help make their testimony relevant. They could write that testimony on the copy of the element.

Other methods of questioning

As well as verbal questioning there are a number of other ways to gather information about a candidate's knowledge.

Questions can be presented in written form in a variety of formats:

O   multiple-choice question papers

O   essays or project reports

O   short-answer tests.

> There is a wide range of methods to gather evidence of a candidate's knowledge.

These methods can be used in any circumstances, but are particularly useful when the knowledge to be tested is complex and broad or when it suits the candidate and organisation.

Other methods which essentially ask questions in an open format, allowing candidates to present evidence of their knowledge, include:

O   work diaries or journals

O   workplace projects or assignments

O   reflective reports or storyboards.

These methods are often less intimidating to candidates and can be motivating mechanisms to encourage candidates in their qualification.

By using a range of flexible methods, candidates have the opportunity to present evidence of their knowledge and understanding to an assessor.

It's difficult to record the evidence gained by questioning. You can develop checklists of questions which will record which questions were asked and the candidate's answers. You can tape record the questioning and the answers. You and the candidate could write short notes on the discussion that took place. Whichever way you choose it is important for you and the candidate to have a record of any questioning. Keeping records of questioning and its results provides you with a record of what happened and the candidate with evidence. There is more information about recording knowledge evidence in Chapter 10 'Recording'.

> Recording knowledge evidence can be difficult.

The method used to gather evidence of a candidate's knowledge by questioning should be selected on the basis of:

O   the candidate's preference

O   the organisational resources and time restraints

O   ensuring sufficient evidence is generated.

> Knowledge evidence will always be necessary to make an overall judgement of competence.
>
> See Chapter 6 'Judging evidence'.

9. GIVING FEEDBACK

THIS CHAPTER IS ABOUT:

○ Feedback

○ The skills of telling candidates your assessment decision.

TDLB STANDARDS

This chapter covers feedback during and after assessment. There are performance criteria in elements D324, D332 and D333 which describe this activity.

The exercises in this section will provide evidence for your portfolio.

THIS CHAPTER WILL HELP YOU TO:

○ Give your assessment decision to candidates in the most effective and encouraging manner.

KEY POINTS

1. When candidates have presented sufficient evidence to demonstrate their competence, assessors need to tell them of this.

2. This feedback should be clear, relevant, constructive and given as soon as is practicable after the event.

3. If candidates are not yet competent, assessors should be clear about what they expect candidates to do, for example, if they need to collect more evidence.

It is important to give feedback to candidates for the following reasons:

○ To let them know when they are successful

○ To keep them involved and motivated

○ To point out when things are wrong

○ To agree arrangements about training or other assessments

○ To give them an opportunity to share in the assessment process.

This section aims to present the important points about feedback by encouraging you to think about feedback situations you have been in.

✴ EXERCISE

Before you look at what feedback is in your role as an assessor, think for a moment what feedback is generally. To do this, list some of the occasions when you have received some sort of feedback, either from friends, relations or colleagues.

I hope you found occasions from all sorts of different situations because, whether we are aware of it or not, we get a lot of feedback all the time.

We get feedback from:

○   the way people look at and talk to us

○   things we touch and smell

○   the result of trying something out

○   the answers to our questions.

✱ EXERCISE

Now go back to the list you made on the previous page and answer these questions for each occasion:

1. How did the feedback affect what you know?

2. How did the feedback affect how you felt?

3. Did the feedback alter what you were about to do?

Important points in answering the previous exercise:

O   It's always best to give feedback as soon as possible after the event

O   Start with the positive. Tell the candidate what he or she did right

O   Ask the candidate how they feel it went. They may be aware of their omission

O   When speaking about something that was left out or went wrong, be clear and direct. Don't try to wrap the problem up in cotton wool or the candidate may not realise what you are saying

O   Don't labour what went wrong. Get the candidate to recognise and identify how it can be corrected in the future

O   Leave the candidate with something positive to do, and suggest and arrange a future opportunity for another assessment

O   Be sensitive about how the candidate feels about their performance

To summarise

Feedback should be:

O   **clear** - making sure the candidate knows what was right and what was wrong

O   **prompt** - given as soon as possible after the event

O   **relevant** - containing comments about the performance in relation to the standards

O   **positive** - always being optimistic and looking for something to praise

O   **constructive** - leaving the candidate with something they can do.

10. RECORDING

THIS CHAPTER IS ABOUT:

O   The basics of recording information in assessment systems

O   What documents are used in vocational assessment

O   Awarding body documentation and in-house designed forms.

THE CHAPTER WILL HELP YOU TO:

O   Complete the documents in your recording system effectively

O   Understand the progression of recording

O   Be aware of different documents and their uses.

KEY POINTS

1.   All documents should be completed clearly, legibly and fully.

2.   Awarding bodies will provide documentation that must be completed.

3.   Your centre or organisation may design forms and documents to support the assessment system.

Each awarding body has different documentation. Centres will have their own recording systems. However, there are some general rules that can be followed to make form filling and record keeping efficient. It is important that information is available to be passed on as necessary and to record a candidate's achievements.

There are some important basic principles for keeping written records:

Write clearly and legibly

This means writing in ballpoint (preferably black to make photocopying clear) at a speed that makes your writing legible. Documents will have to be read by other people and may have to be photocopied.

Don't use abbreviations or shortened forms

Many of us have a shorthand when writing, consisting of acronyms and abbreviations. Others may not understand these so it is a good principle to write things in full.

Give full information in records

Unless specified, ticks and 'yes' or 'no' answers don't offer sufficient information. In your recording use specific examples of events, places and dates.

Take responsibility for your recording

Although paperwork can be tedious, the recording and documentation system in vocational qualifications is essential for candidates to be certificated. Records have to be signed, often by you and the candidate, and some will have to be countersigned.

What documents?

All vocational assessment systems will have a document to record the assessor's final decision to recognise competence in a candidate. This may be an awarding body document or have been produced by the organisation and approved by the awarding body.

Different awarding bodies have different names for this document such as candidate's log, record of achievement or assessment record. The purpose of the document is to record when a candidate reaches competence in an element and the types of evidence accepted for recognising that competence.

As elements of competence are assessed, units are achieved and eventually all the units for a qualification will be complete. The document is a record of how a candidate has achieved competence in the qualification, and forms the basis of any checks by internal verifiers who maintain the quality and consistency of assessments made by assessors.

TO DO !

Check the awarding body documentation you will need to complete as an assessor and make sure that you understand its purpose, layout and how to complete it.

Make a copy of these documents and make notes on their completion and purpose.

Keep this copy in your portfolio.

TDLB STANDARDS

The two TO DO exercises provide evidence of your knowledge and understanding of the recording system and will be useful evidence for elements D324 and D333.

To support this final record, centres may design in-house documents which record evidence of a candidate's competence. These documents may include observation checklists, question checklists, observation reports, action plans and candidate records and portfolios.

The purpose of these records is to aid the information flow and evidence recording. Such records also keep track of a candidate's progress towards a qualification.

Examples of these documents are included in Chapters 11 and 12. Each centre will have forms and documents which suit its own needs.

TO DO !

Check the documentation that your centre has designed. Get a copy of each document, make notes on its purpose and its place in the recording system.

Include these copies in your portfolio.

Confidentiality

Documents must be securely stored so that the confidentiality of candidates is maintained. Awarding bodies need to be assured that there is a secure place where documents are kept. Assessors must ensure that they do not leave assessment documentation lying around where it can be openly seen and read.

The following two chapters give worked examples of the assessment process with a candidate, and illustrate the use of various documents at various stages of the assessment process.

11. A WORKED EXAMPLE OF THE NVQ ASSESSMENT PROCESS

This chapter illustrates how a candidate might go through the NVQ assessment process. The example is based on the stages of the process outlined in the diagram opposite. Although the details of the process may vary from the way your organisation arranges assessments, the fundamental stages will be the same.

By following this worked example you will be able to:

O   get an overview of the whole process

O   identify where specific skills and procedures, explained in the text, fit into the process

O   see examples of completed documents.

TDLB STANDARDS
There are no specific links in this chapter to the TDLB standards. The chapter is designed to illustrate the process of assessment and how assessment skills are put into practice.

The following chapter presents an example of how a candidate goes through the GNVQ assessment process.

An example of the GNVQ process is presented in the following Chapter 12.

Setting the scene

Claire is an office supervisor in a large open-plan office of a large manufacturing company. For two years the company has been offering NVQs to its employees as part of its quality performance policy and as a way of qualifying the workforce. Brian joined the company after a series of other administrative jobs but had never taken any qualifications before. After an period of induction, Brian is encouraged to consider taking an NVQ in administration.

How a candidate goes through the NVQ assessment process

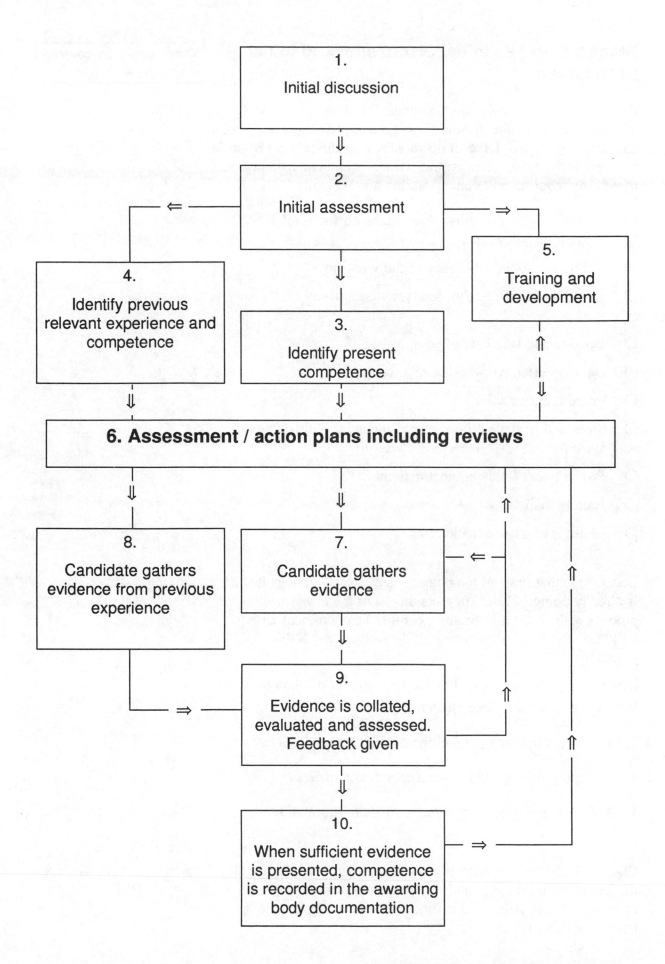

1.
Initial discussion

2.
Initial assessment

4.
Identify previous relevant experience and competence

3.
Identify present competence

5.
Training and development

6. Assessment / action plans including reviews

8.
Candidate gathers evidence from previous experience

7.
Candidate gathers evidence

9.
Evidence is collated, evaluated and assessed. Feedback given

10.
When sufficient evidence is presented, competence is recorded in the awarding body documentation

Stages 1 and 2. Initial discussion and initial assessment

These stages are covered in Chapter 3.

Brian agrees to look at the units in a level 1 NVQ in administration. Claire spends some time explaining about NVQs and what Brian will have to do to gain a qualification. Brian is relieved to find that there are no written examinations and much of what is required will come from his normal work.

Claire shows Brian the units which make up the level 1 NVQ in administration. These are:

○ Contribute to the efficiency of the work flow

○ Contribute to the health, safety and security of the workplace

○ Operate and take care of equipment

○ Develop effective working relationships

○ Process information

○ Store and retrieve information using an established storage system

○ Produce text following instructions

○ Handle mail

○ Monitor and issue stock items.

Brian finds that most of the units contain work activities that he is already doing. Claire suggests they start the assessment process with a unit that Brian is familiar and confident with to build up step-by-step, covering all the units of the NVQ gradually.

Brian decides to start with unit L1.5 - Process information.

In this unit there are three elements:

1.5.1 Process incoming and outgoing telecommunications

1.5.2 Supply information to meet specified requests

1.5.3 Check and process routine, numerical information.

Claire asks Brian to complete a self-assessment exercise for all the elements in this unit, and his completed form is presented opposite. Claire will use this form as the basis for discussing Brian's action plan.

Brian's completed self-assessment for unit L1.5 in the administration standards

Name	Organisation
Brian Goodman	**Pica Promotions**

Unit title:	Date: *6 April*	Unit No.: L1.5

Process information

Unit topics

Using the telephone and fax

Taking and transmitting messages

Relaying information

Writing memos, messages and short reports

Company style and procedure

Customer service

Presenting information

Examples of evidence

Memos, letters, short reports and written messages

Work diary or log of performance

Observation in the workplace of:

O Approved organisation telephone manner

O Taking and giving messages

O Presenting information

O Processing misdirected calls and wrong numbers

Testimony from supervisors and colleagues

Fault report procedures and documents

Elements	A	B	C	D	E
1.5.1 Process incoming and outgoing telecommunications	✔				✔
1.5.2 Supply information to meet specified requests		✔	✔		
1.5.3 Check and process routine, numerical information	✔				

LEGEND

A - I do this now as part of my work and, according to the standards, can identify evidence of my competence.

B - I do this now and feel that I am competent according to the standards but I am unsure of gathering evidence.

C - I do this now but am unsure of my competence according to the standards.

D - I am unsure how to do this work activity.

E - I have done this in the past and can offer evidence of recent performance according to the standards.

Possible strategies

Gather evidence and present to the assessor - probably supported by workplace observation.

Support and advice in identifying and gathering evidence supplemented by workplace observation.

As for B but possibly with some additional training and practice.

Plan training and development.

Gather evidence and present to assessor. Make plans for the assessment of present performance.

Brian's self-assessment indicates that he is confident of his competence in all the elements of unit L1.5. Claire has worked alongside Brian and knows his supervisor. She knows that Brian's self-assessment is realistic.

Stages 3, 4 and 5

Brian's ticks in columns A and B of his self-assessment show that he is identifying his present competence (Stage 3). For element 1.5.2, he may require guidance about gathering evidence but this can be identified in the assessment plan. The ticks in column E show that he can identify previous relevant experience (Stage 4) from a previous employer. Brian is confident of his ability in the work activities of unit L1.5, so at this stage there is no need to plan any training and development (Stage 5). It is possible that in the course of assessments Brian may need training in some aspects of the standards, in which case it can then be included in the action plan.

Claire suggests that Brian begins to gather evidence of his competence in unit L1.5, one element at a time.

She asks him to look at element 1.5.1 and think of occasions when the performance criteria in the element occur in the workplace.

Element 1.5.1 is presented in Chapter 5, page 32.

Brian can identify where his job fits the performance criteria. He and Claire discuss examples of evidence that occur in the routine of work, for example memos and messages, telephone and fax logs and reports that Brian has presented to his supervisor.

Claire also checks that the scope of Brian's job covers all aspects of the range statement. The office has an outside line and Brian regularly uses this and transfers calls around the internal system.

Brian has done this sort of work recently in another office. He has a telephone and fax log that he kept there and also a customer care certificate from his previous employer. Claire acknowledges this and asks Brian to bring them to the next action planning session. This previous evidence may be difficult to relate to the standards but can be taken into account when making an overall judgement about competence.

> The criteria used to judge this evidence from a previous employer are covered in Chapter 6, 'Judging evidence'.

Claire and Brian agree that the main source of evidence is available from the workplace and start to construct an action plan on how to collect it.

Chapter 5 covers identifying and recognising evidence. Making an assessment plan is the application of those principles to an individual candidate, his or her work situation and needs.

Stage 6. Action plans and assessment plans

Claire and Brian discuss the evidence Brian can collect from his workplace. The general agreements are written on Brian's action plan, presented below.

As well as agreeing the general actions, Claire and Brian agree to meet again a month later to review progress.

ACTION PLAN

Name: **Brian Goodman**

Award/qualification: **Administration NVQ level 1**

DATE	ACTIONS AGREED	REVIEW DATE
8 April	**Brian is going to collect evidence for element 1.5.1 in the normal course of work and get in touch with his previous employer.**	**9 May**

This action plan only notes general actions and agreements. Claire and Brian use the assessment plan to identify specific examples of evidence that Brian will collect. The assessment plan that Claire and Brian agree for element 1.5.1 is reproduced overleaf.

As well as evidence from present performance, Brian has agreed to gather evidence from his previous employment. The assessment plan gives more detail of the evidence Claire and Brian have agreed to consider.

Stages 7 and 8. Gathering evidence

Brian is now clear about the evidence he has to collect. He spends the month to the next review gathering that evidence.

ASSESSMENT PLAN

Element No.: *L1.5.1*

Element Title: *Process incoming and outgoing telecommunications*

Evidence I can produce from previous experience.

Telephone and fax log from my previous employer, Relish Sales

Customer care certificate from training at Relish Sales

Evidence I could gather from present performance.

Observation by Claire in my workplace

Documents: memos, messages, short reports, fault log

Company procedures and policies with notes on how I use them

Witness testimony from colleagues and clients

Self-report on the disclosure of information

Activities, training and plans to generate and gather the full range of evidence.

At the next review, verbal questioning by Claire to cover all aspects of the standards

Note these plans on the assessment / action plan and cross-reference to other elements when evidence can be used for a number of different elements.

Chapter 6 covers judging evidence and Chapter 9 looks at the skills of feedback.

Stage 9. Evidence is collated, evaluated and assessed. Feedback given. (Review of the action plan)

At the date agreed on the action plan (9 May), Claire and Brian meet again to check on Brian's progress.

Claire uses the criteria for judging evidence that were presented in Chapter 6.

VACS

Is the evidence: Valid, Authentic, Current and Sufficient?

A portfolio is the method of collecting and presenting evidence for assessment.

Appendix 3 gives more details and guidance on the structure of a portfolio.

In this case Brian has been able to gather sufficient evidence including documents, reports, activities and Claire's observation and questioning. Brian has collected this evidence in a portfolio and referenced the evidence to element 1.5.1.

The structure of Brian's portfolio is outlined overleaf.

The next step is to go back to the action plan. Claire and Brian agree to move on to element 1.5.2 and their decisions about evidence are similar to those for 1.5.1. The next stage of the action plan is as follows:

ACTION PLAN

Name: **Brian Goodman**

Award/qualification: **Administration NVQ level 1**

DATE	ACTIONS AGREED	REVIEW DATE
8 April	**Brian is going to collect evidence for element 1.5.1 in the normal course of work and get in touch with his previous employer.**	**9 May**
9 May	**Brian presented sufficient evidence for 1.5.1. He now has an assessment plan identifying evidence for 1.5.2.**	**31 May**

THE STRUCTURE OF BRIAN'S PORTFOLIO

Brian is using an A4 ring binder as his portfolio.

Guidance on the structure of portfolios is given in Appendix 3.

In this ring binder is a brief section for information about himself including address, place of work, assessor's name, NVQ award and registration number. This information is contained on a single sheet.

The next section of the portfolio contains a brief résumé of Brian's work experience. It is not a full CV going back over all his working life but rather a record of work experience with recent employers. Details of the work experience are targeted to the work activities of the standards in the NVQ. For two recent office jobs Brian explains his work responsibilities and activities. Brian explains that he is also secretary of a local darts club and feels that this experience may be useful sometime in assessment. This information is contained on two sheets.

Brief factual details and a work résumé covering experience that is relevant to the standards in the qualification.

Next in the portfolio comes a copy of all the standards in the NVQ. There is a page for each element so this section contains about forty sheets.

A copy of the standards which also acts as a structure to keep evidence.

Brian uses the structure of the standards to order and keep his evidence. As he fills in self-assessment sheets and gathers evidence for particular elements he keeps those papers behind that element page in the standards. This way means that Brian and his assessor can relate evidence to performance criteria.

Self-assessment sheets, action plans and assessment plans.

At the back of his portfolio Brian keeps a work diary which cross-references to pieces of evidence. This way Brian's diary can be used as another source of evidence linked to particular standards and events.

A work diary provides a good way to link activities to dates and allows Brian to write reflective reports on what he has done.

Eventually Brian's ring binder may get too full and he may have to use a lever arch file.

In addition to his portfolio, Brian and Claire keep the awarding body documents up-to-date as a record of achievement and progress (these documents are supplied by the awarding body and can be called candidate log, candidate pack, record of achievement, assessment record or candidate record). Brian's own portfolio acts as a supporting document to this official documentation.

The portfolio supplements the summative recording documentation required by the awarding body.

Chapter 10 covers the documents and skills needed in recording competence.

Stage 10. Recording competence

After a series of reviews, Brian has been assessed as competent in all the elements of unit L1.5. Claire can record Brian's competence in the awarding body documentation. This document records summative achievement of competence and is only completed when successful assessments have been made for a whole unit.

Different awarding bodies have differing formats for their documents but all have a place to record the completion of a unit that usually needs to be signed by the assessor and the candidate.

As Brian and Claire work through the NVQ element by element, unit by unit, eventually there will come a time when Brian has been assessed as competent in all units of the NVQ. Brian's portfolio will contain the evidence to support the assessment judgements made by Claire.

See Chapter 2 for details of roles and functions within the assessment team.

At this stage the evidence must be verified, firstly by the organisation's own verifier (the internal verifier), and secondly by the awarding body verifier (the external verifier). The purpose of this exercise is to ensure that the process of assessment carried out by the assessor is correct and that judgements made by the assessor are competent and consistent with the interpretation of the standards. Internal and external verifiers will not look at every item of evidence. They check a sample of all aspects of the assessment process to ensure that assessments are being carried out to the quality specified by the awarding body.

When the documentation is complete the centre can apply for Brian's certificate, which will duly arrive from the awarding body.

12. A WORKED EXAMPLE OF THE GNVQ ASSESSMENT PROCESS

This chapter illustrates how a candidate might go through the GNVQ assessment process. The example is based on the stages of the process outlined in the diagram opposite. Although the details of the process may vary from the way your organisation arranges assessments, the stages will be fundamentally the same.

By following this worked example you will be able to:

○ get an overview of the whole assessment process

○ identify where specific skills and procedures, explained in the text, fit into the process

○ see examples of completed documents.

> **TDLB STANDARDS**
>
> There are no specific links in this chapter to the TDLB standards. The chapter is designed to illustrate the process of assessment and how assessment skills are put into practice.

Setting the scene

Jo is a school teacher of GNVQ business. Pat is a 17-year-old studying A-level pure mathematics as well as GNVQ advanced business. This example looks at the three elements: 'Investigate administrative systems', 'Investigate communication systems' and 'Investigate information processing systems'.

> This example uses three elements from the GNVQ advanced business. More details of one of these elements appear in Chapter 5 where it was used to illustrate examples of evidence.

Stages 1 and 2. Initial discussion and initial assessment

The two principles which should guide delivery models for the GNVQ are that they allow progression for the candidate and enhance his or her learning programme without replicating work being done elsewhere.

Learning programmes are not prescribed by the awarding body. Centres are free to design their own and are encouraged to draw as widely as possible on available resources within and outside the centre.

How a candidate goes through the GNVQ assessment process

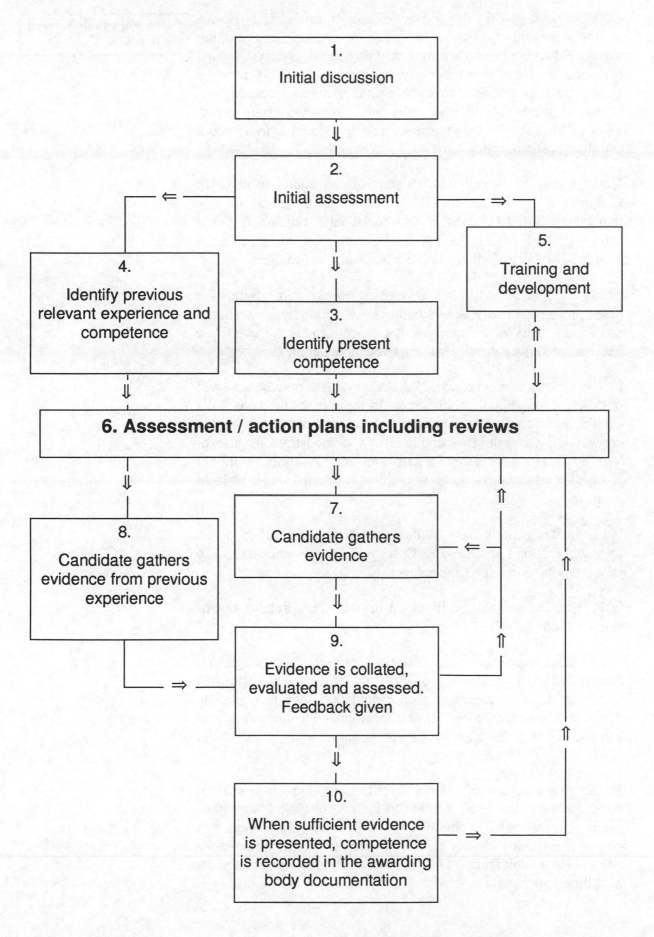

Stages 1 and 2 *continued*

GNVQs are based on the active learning of candidates. Active learning demands the use of a variety of teaching and learning styles. When beginning a unit it may be helpful to have a formal presentation from a teacher or visiting speaker. It may be appropriate to present research from printed, recorded and computer materials. Visits, interviews, surveys, group work, work shadowing, work experience and individual activity work can then be introduced.

These stages are covered in Chapter 3.

GNVQs may be linked with existing qualifications so that, for example, a candidate on GNVQ advanced business takes a language AS level. Health and social care candidates could follow an NVQ unit in care at level 2 such as 'Contribute to the on-going support of clients and others significant to them'.

Most candidates will be developing their core skills for assessment and ideally be generating evidence through vocational activities. This is an integrated approach so that a candidate learns core skills naturally within a vocational context.

In some cases, however, core skills achievement may be assessed outside the vocational programme. In these cases the core skills should be offered and assessed in an activity with a vocational context. For example a candidate may demonstrate the use of 'Application of number' in a part-time job. Assessment should always be in a realistic context and not conducted as an isolated exercise.

If candidates already have skills at or above the level to which they are working in the GNVQ they should be encouraged to take the core skills at a higher level.

GNVQ candidates will be involved in individual programmes of activity learning.

Sometimes teaching teams develop projects for diagnostic assessment of candidates, collaborating to reach a consensus about development needs of each candidate. They then use the diagnostic assessment to adjust the emphasis of teaching and learning during the rest of the programme to suit individual needs.

Jo has given details of all the GNVQ units and discussed the structure and terms used in them to the twelve GNVQ advanced business candidates including Pat. The teaching team has prepared activities closely related to performance criteria, range and evidence indicators. The procedure for developing activities is outlined opposite.

Developing an appropriate activity for assessment of GNVQs

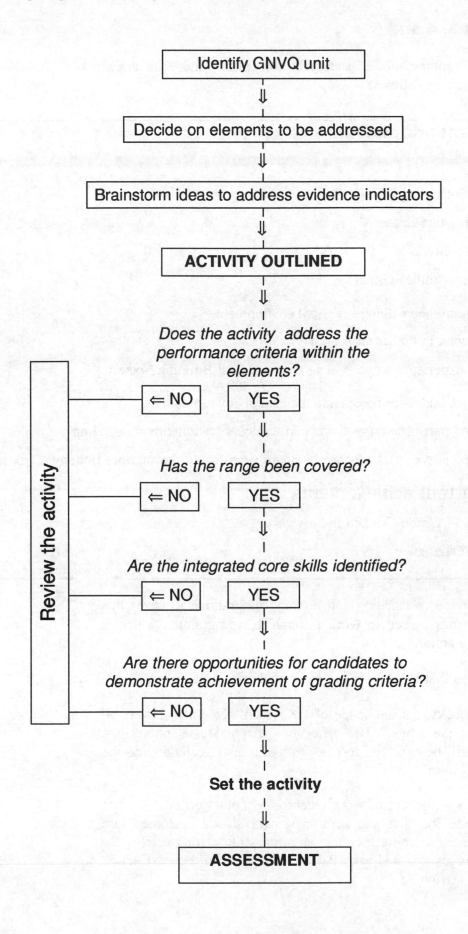

Identify GNVQ unit

⇓

Decide on elements to be addressed

⇓

Brainstorm ideas to address evidence indicators

⇓

ACTIVITY OUTLINED

⇓

Does the activity address the performance criteria within the elements?

⇐ NO   YES

⇓

Has the range been covered?

⇐ NO   YES

⇓

Are the integrated core skills identified?

⇐ NO   YES

⇓

Are there opportunities for candidates to demonstrate achievement of grading criteria?

⇐ NO   YES

⇓

Set the activity

⇓

ASSESSMENT

Review the activity

Stages 3, 4 and 5

Pat had completed a statement of prior and concurrent achievement as follows:

Relevant prior learning

GCSEs

English language Grade C

Mathematics Grade A

Science Grade B

Business studies Grade C

Other experience within the school environment

IT lessons in the lower school

Work experience in year 11 at City and East Building Society

Experience and learning outside the school environment

Worked part-time on Saturdays in the local Nationwide video shop

Worked at the local Electricity Board shop for all the summer holidays

Concurrent achievements

GCSE IT Grade C taken in November

Work experience

Jo has devised a teaching and learning programme to cover this unit. Pat has agreed to work through this programme which is part of the action plan.

Jo suggests that Pat begins to gather evidence.

Jo also checks that the scope of Pat's work placement covers all aspects of the range. The office has an outside telephone line and Pat will be expected to use this and transfer calls around the internal system.

Pat has done this sort of work recently in another office. She has a telephone log that she kept there and also a customer care certificate for a training course she did while at that office. Jo acknowledges this and asks Pat to bring them to the next action planning session.

Stage 6. Action plans and assessment plans

Jo and Pat discuss the evidence Pat can collect from her work placement. The general agreements are written on Pat's action plan, presented below.

As well as agreeing the general actions, Jo and Pat agree to meet again a month later to review progress.

ACTION PLAN

Name: *Pat Barker*

Award/qualification: *GNVQ business - advanced*

DATE	ACTIONS AGREED	REVIEW DATE
1 June	*Over the period of your work placement keep a log or diary of the activities that you are involved in. Relate these activities to the performance criteria and the range in the standards. For each entry you must ensure that someone confirms what you have done and ask them to comment on your performance.*	*1 July*

This action plan only notes general actions and agreements. Jo and Pat use an assessment plan to identify specific examples of evidence that Pat will generate. The assessment plan that Jo and Pat agree for elements 2.1, 2.2 and 2.3 is reproduced overleaf.

As well as evidence from present performance, Pat has agreed to gather evidence from her previous employment. The assessment plan gives more detail of the evidence Jo and Pat have agreed to consider.

Stages 7 and 8. Gathering evidence

Pat is now clear about the evidence she has to collect. She spends the month to the next review gathering that evidence.

ASSESSMENT PLAN

Element nos: *2.1, 2.2, 2.3*

Element titles:

Investigate administration systems

Investigate communication systems

Investigate information systems

Evidence from previous experience.

Worked part-time on Saturdays in the local Nationwide video shop

Worked at the local Electricity Board shop for all the summer holiday

Work experience in year 11 at City and East Building Society

Evidence from previous telephone logs and customer care training

---

Evidence from present performance.

In first week prepare an account of the administration system in the organisation showing how the needs of the organisation are met

Evidence will be produced for unit 2 business systems elements 1, 2 and 3

Evidence will be produced for the following core elements: Communications 3.1, 3.2, 3.3 and 3.4

These activities are likely to produce evidence for grading

Activities, teaching and plans to generate and gather the full range of evidence.

Activities as above

Teaching in accordance with the business GNVQ programme

Note these plans on the assessment / action plan and cross-reference to other elements when evidence can be used for a number of different elements.

Stage 9. Evidence is collated, evaluated and assessed. Feedback given. (Review of the action plan)

At the date agreed on the action plan (1 July), Jo and Pat meet again to check on Pat's progress.

VACS

Jo uses the criteria for judging evidence that were presented in Chapter 6.

Is the evidence: Valid, Authentic, Current and Sufficient?

A portfolio is the method of collecting and presenting evidence for assessment.

Appendix 3 gives more details and guidance on the structure of a portfolio.

In this case Pat has been able to gather sufficient evidence, including documents, reports, activities and Jo's questioning. Pat has collected this evidence in a portfolio and referenced the evidence to elements 2.1, 2.2 and 2.3.

The structure of Pat's portfolio is outlined opposite.

The next step is to prepare a further action plan. Jo and Pat agree to move on to elements 3.1 and 3.2 and their decisions about evidence are similar to those for unit 2. The next stage of the action plan is as follows:

ACTION PLAN

Name: *Pat Barker*

Award/qualification: *GNVQ business - advanced*

DATE	ACTIONS AGREED	REVIEW DATE
1 June	*Over the period of your work placement keep a log or diary of the activities that you are involved in. Relate these activities to the performance criteria and the range in the standards. For each entry you must ensure that someone confirms what you have done and ask them to comment on your performance.*	*1 July*
1 July	*Pat presented sufficient evidence for 2.1, 2.2 and 2.3. She now has an assessment plan identifying evidence for 3.1 and 3.2.*	*3 August*

THE STRUCTURE OF PAT'S PORTFOLIO

Pat is using an A4 ring binder as her portfolio.

In this ring binder is a brief section for background information including name, candidate number, centre name and number, assessor's name, GNVQ vocational area and level of award. This information is contained on a single sheet.

> Guidance on the structure of portfolios is given in Appendix 3.

The next section of the portfolio contains a brief résumé of Pat's experience. It is not a full CV but rather a record of work experience with recent employers. Details of the work experience are targeted to the activities in the standards in the GNVQ. For two recent office work placements Pat explains her work responsibilities and activities. Pat explains that she is also secretary of a local community club and feels that this experience may be useful sometime in assessment. This information is contained on two sheets.

> Brief factual details and a work résumé covering experience that is relevant to the standards in the qualification.

Pat uses the structure of the standards to order and keep her evidence. As she completes assessment plans and gathers evidence for particular elements she keeps those documents together which means that Pat and her assessor can relate evidence to performance criteria.

> Action plans, assessment plans and evidence.

At the back of her portfolio Pat keeps a work diary which cross-references to pieces of evidence. This way Pat's diary can be used as another source of evidence linked to particular standards and events.

> A work diary provides a good way to link activities to dates and allows Pat to write reflective reports on what she has done.

Eventually Pat's ring binder may get too full and she may have to use a lever arch file.

In addition to her portfolio, Jo and Pat keep the awarding body documents up-to-date as a record of achievement and progress (these documents are supplied by the awarding body and can be called candidate log, candidate pack, record of achievement, assessment record or candidate record). Pat's own portfolio acts as a supporting document to this official documentation.

Stage 10. Recording competence

After a series of reviews, Pat has been assessed as competent in all the elements of unit 2. Jo can record Pat's competence in the awarding body documentation. This document records summative achievement of competence and is only completed when successful assessments have been made for a whole unit.

Different awarding bodies have differing formats for their documents but all have a place to record the completion of a unit that usually needs to be signed by the assessor and the candidate.

As Pat and Jo work through the GNVQ element by element, unit by unit, eventually there will come a time when Pat has been assessed as competent in all units of the GNVQ. Pat's portfolio will contain the evidence to support the assessment judgements made by Jo.

See Chapter 2 for details of roles and functions within the assessment team.

At this stage the evidence must be verified, firstly by the organisation's own verifier (the internal verifier), and secondly by the awarding body verifier (the external verifier). The purpose of this exercise is to ensure that the assessment process has been carried out as required by the awarding body. Internal and external verifiers will not look at every item of evidence. They check a sample of all aspects of the assessment process to ensure that assessments are being carried out to the quality specified by the awarding body.

When the documentation is complete the centre can apply for Pat's certificate, which will duly arrive from the awarding body.

13. LANGUAGE AND TERMS

This chapter explains some of the terms used in assessing vocational qualifications. It will be useful as you work through the book. Cross-references to other chapters in the workbook are given where appropriate. The explanations of these terms are not meant to provide comprehensive definitions but rather a working explanation. Comprehensive definitions can be found in literature from awarding bodies and the National Council for Vocational Qualifications (NCVQ).

ACCREDITATION OF PRIOR LEARNING (APL)

An attractive characteristic of vocational qualifications is that candidates can be credited for what they can do already. A candidate can present evidence of previous experience which assessors can take into account in judging present competence. This procedure is known as accreditation of prior learning. Evidence of prior learning may come from previous work situations (paid and unpaid), social experience, training programmes or qualification certificates. These sources of evidence must be carefully judged prior to final interview, when competence is confirmed. This procedure is also known as: Accreditation of Prior Experience (APE) and Accreditation of Prior Achievement (APA). Most awarding bodies and lead bodies give guidance on these procedures.

> See Chapter 5 on identifying and recognising evidence and Chapter 6 on judging evidence, with special reference to evidence from previous experience.

ACTION PLAN

This is a plan negotiated between a candidate and an assessor to identify how the candidate will go through the award. The action plan may include arrangements for training, assessment or gathering evidence from prior learning.
(See also ASSESSMENT PLAN)

> See Chapters 11 and 12 for examples.

APPROVED ASSESSMENT CENTRE

Any centre offering vocational qualifications must have the approval of an awarding body, which itself has been accredited by NCVQ. Approval of centres follows a common procedure and requires the centre to assure the awarding body that the centre has trained staff, correct administration and assessment procedures and an appeals and anti-discriminatory policy. A centre can be a single organisation, a geographic location or a consortium of smaller units.
(See also AWARDING BODY)

> See the section 'How do candidates achieve a vocational qualification?' in Chapter 4.

ASSESSMENT

The process of judging evidence of competence against specified criteria. In vocational assessment, evidence is used to judge competence and the specified criteria are derived from national standards.
(See also COMPETENCE-BASED ASSESSMENT)

ASSESSMENT GUIDANCE
(See STRUCTURE OF NATIONAL STANDARDS)

ASSESSMENT PLAN

See Chapters 11 and 12 for examples.

A recorded agreement between the candidate and assessor to clarify what is to be assessed, when assessment will take place and what evidence may be gathered. A number of assessment plans may be part of an action plan providing more detailed information on assessments that will take place.
(See also ACTION PLAN)

ASSESSOR

See Chapter 2 and the section in Chapter 4, 'Who is involved?'.

This is the person who assesses candidates taking a vocational qualification. Assessors may be work colleagues, trainers or teachers. The purpose of this workbook is to prepare assessors for their role in vocational assessment.

Other role titles sometimes used include work-based assessor, skills assessor and vocational assessor.

AWARDING BODY

See the section 'How do candidates achieve a vocational qualification?' in Chapter 4.

Most awarding bodies have a history of examining and validation. They are accredited by NCVQ to award specific vocational qualifications. Awarding bodies establish assessment procedures. A centre wishing to offer a vocational qualification must be approved by an awarding body accredited for that qualification. A particular vocational qualification may be offered by a number of awarding bodies.
(See also APPROVED ASSESSMENT CENTRE)

CANDIDATE

See the section 'Who is involved?' in Chapter 4.

This is the person taking a vocational qualification. Candidates register with a centre approved to offer a particular qualification and are provided with the necessary support to achieve a vocational qualification.

CANDIDATE LOG

See Chapter 10 on recording.

This is a booklet, usually provided by the awarding body, which provides a way of recording a candidate's achievement of competence. It contains places for assessors and verifiers to sign and is used to initiate certification from the awarding body.

The candidate log is also known as record of achievement, assessment record, candidate pack and candidate record by different awarding bodies.

COMPETENCE-BASED ASSESSMENT

The assessment of NVQs and GNVQs uses criteria laid down within national standards of competence, accredited by NCVQ. The assessments are based on evidence presented by the candidate.

ELEMENT OF COMPETENCE

(See STRUCTURE OF NATIONAL STANDARDS)

EVIDENCE

Evidence of competent performance is of two types: performance and supplementary or supporting. It can come from a variety of sources including observation of performance, products, questioning and testimonies.

Assessors will need to see valid, authentic, current and sufficient evidence before a candidate can be awarded a unit of competence.

> See Chapter 3 for a summary of the types and sources of evidence and Chapter 5 for more details of the sources.

EXTERNAL VERIFIER (EV)

This is a person appointed by an awarding body to advise and approve centres and maintain a quality monitoring role. External verifiers will visit centres and verify assessment practice and centre procedures.

> See Chapter 2 for the external verifier's part in the assessment team.

GENERAL NATIONAL VOCATIONAL QUALIFICATIONS (GNVQs)

These qualifications are part of the national framework of vocational qualifications introduced by the government. GNVQs are designed for delivery in educational establishments and are designed to provide a vocational qualification route as an alternative or in addition to GCSEs and A levels. GNVQs will be available at three levels: foundation, intermediate and advanced. Like NVQs, GNVQs are specified as outcomes, and have the same structure and assessment methods. Students holding GNVQs will have achieved a foundation of general skills, knowledge and understanding which underpins a range of occupations.

> For more detail see Chapter 4 and a worked example in Chapter 12.

INTERNAL VERIFIER (IV)

This is a member of the assessment team who has responsibility for ensuring assessments carried out by assessors are consistent and to the required standard. The IV normally countersigns the assessment documentation and liaises with the awarding body on behalf of the centre.

> See Chapter 2 for the internal verifier's part in the assessment team.

LEAD BODY

This body represents the wide interests within an employment sector. It is responsible for developing national standards of competence and associated NVQs. There are nearly 200 lead bodies representing sectors such as: care, retailing, accountancy, animal care, and training and development. There is to be some rationalisation of these lead bodies into Occupational Standards Councils (OSCs) during 1994 and 1995.

NATIONAL COUNCIL FOR VOCATIONAL QUALIFICATIONS (NCVQ)

This body was established by government to lead and oversee the reform of vocational qualifications in England, Wales and Northern Ireland. It accredits national standards and qualifications within an overall framework covering all aspects of work activity and vocational qualifications.

NATIONAL VOCATIONAL QUALIFICATION (NVQ)

For more detail see Chapter 4.

An NVQ can be defined as a group of units which have relevance to employment. An NVQ covers a range of functions which may be broader than a person's job. The standards for an NVQ are developed by a lead body and endorsed by the NCVQ. NVQs are awarded by an awarding body (such as City and Guilds) to candidates who have been assessed as competent against the national standards.

(See also UNIT CERTIFICATION)

NVQ LEVEL

For more explanation and detail of levels see Chapters 3 and 4.

NVQs are accredited at a particular qualification level from 1 to 5. These levels have been established by NCVQ as reflecting the complexity of activities, amount of supervision received and scope of the work activities included in an NVQ. Level 1 qualifications cover competence in the performance of a range of varied work activities, most of which are routine and predictable. Level 4 qualifications cover competence in a broad range of complex, technical or professional work activities performed in a wide variety of contexts and with a substantial degree of personal responsibility and autonomy. Responsibility for the work of others and the allocation of resources are often included.

PERFORMANCE CRITERIA

(See STRUCTURE OF NATIONAL STANDARDS)

PORTFOLIO

This can be a folder, box, file or stack of paper but should consist of:

○ basic information about the candidate (name, approved assessment centre, qualification and so on)

○ a brief résumé of previous and present experience

○ a set of standards

○ a place to keep evidence in a clear and structured way.

Candidates are required to accumulate evidence in a systematic and effective manner. Assessors should guide candidates and make comments about the sufficiency of evidence. Internal verifiers also find a structured portfolio easier to check. Most awarding bodies and lead bodies give guidance on portfolio production.

> See Appendix 3 for examples and formats.
>
> Chapters 11 and 12 describe how a portfolio is used.

RANGE STATEMENT

(See STRUCTURE OF NATIONAL STANDARDS)

REVIEWING

This is the process of checking that the points and activities agreed and recorded in an action plan have been completed. It requires regular meetings over agreed time spans to confirm achievement and make new plans.

> See Chapters 11 and 12 for an example of the review process.

STRUCTURE OF NATIONAL STANDARDS

National standards are made up of the following components (see also the explanation and diagram in Chapter 4, page 23):

Unit of competence: This is the main subdivision of statements of competence and describes an area of activity (e.g. Data processing, Monitor and control the use of resources, Enable clients to eat and drink, Business systems). A unit is the smallest part of the competence standards for which a certificate can be awarded (unit certification) and a given number of units make up the award of a particular NVQ or GNVQ. Units of competence include elements of competence, performance criteria and range statements.

> Assessors and candidates need to be familiar with the structure of national standards.
>
> Chapter 4 covers the assessor's job of explaining the structure to candidates.

STRUCTURE OF NATIONAL STANDARDS *continued*

Element of competence: This is the first subdivision of a unit of competence. An element describes a smaller area of work activity (e.g. Update records in a computerised database, Investigate communication systems). An element of competence includes performance criteria, range statements and usually has additional guidance on assessment, evidence or knowledge.

Performance criteria: Performance criteria are evaluative statements describing observable behaviours which make up competent performance (e.g. Operating and safety procedures are followed at all times). They are worded to describe the outcome of that performance. These criteria provide the maximum level of detail which assessors must use to judge competence.

Range statement: These statements define the range of contexts over which competence is assessed. Conditions may include work environments, equipment or customers and clients. Assessors must ensure that candidates can perform in all aspects of the range.

Assessment guidance: Although not a part of the statement of competence, lead bodies and awarding bodies are encouraged to provide guidance about assessment, evidence and the knowledge required for competent performance. This guidance appears under different headings within different standards (e.g. supporting evidence, guidance to assessors, knowledge and understanding, evidence indicators, etc.).

TRAINING AND DEVELOPMENT LEAD BODY (TDLB)

The TDLB standards for assessors are presented in detail in Appendix 1.

This is the lead body responsible for national standards for training and development. The units for assessors and verifiers are part of TDLB national standards.

UNIT CERTIFICATION

A unit of competence is the minimum part of the national standards for which a certificate can be awarded - certification of unit credit.

UNIT OF COMPETENCE

(See STRUCTURE OF NATIONAL STANDARDS)

VACS

See Chapter 6 for details of these criteria.

The mnemonic to remember the criteria used to judge evidence. Valid - Authentic - Current - Sufficient.

VERIFICATION

See Chapter 2 on how quality is maintained by the assessment team.

The process of checking all that should happen in the assessment process is actually happening. Internal verifiers from the organisation and external verifiers from the awarding body ensure the quality of the assessments by sampling the judgements and performance of assessors.

Appendix 1 TDLB units D32 and D33

The diagram shows how the information in the standards is presented.

Unit

D33   Assess Candidate Using Differing Sources of Evidence

Element

D331   Agree and review an assessment plan

Performance Criteria

a   possible opportunities for collecting evidence are identified and evaluated against their relevance to the element(s) to be assessed and their appropriateness to the candidate's needs

b   evidence collection is planned to make effective use of time and resources

c   the opportunities selected provide access to fair and reliable assessment

d   the proposed assessment plan is discussed and agreed with the candidate and others who may be affected

e   if there is disagreement with the proposed assessment plan, options open to the candidate are explained clearly and constructively

f   the assessment plan specifies the target element(s), the opportunities for efficient evidence collection, the assessment methods, the timing of assessments and the arrangements for reviewing the plan

g   requirements to assure the authenticity, reliability and sufficiency of evidence are identified

h   plans are reviewed and updated at agreed times to reflect the candidate's progress within the qualification

Range Statements

1   Opportunities for collecting evidence from
Natural performance; simulations; projects and assignments; questioning; candidate and peer reports; candidate's prior achievement and learning

2   Evidence used for
Own judgements; judgements by other people

3   Candidates
Experienced in presenting evidence; inexperienced in presenting evidence
Candidates with special assessment requirements

The Unit Title
This describes the outcome of achieving the elements that are grouped together to form the unit.

The Element Title
One of the elements that make up the unit. The element title describes what the individual should achieve - in this case an agreed assessment plan.

Performance criteria
In this element, there are eight criteria used to judge performance in achieving the element title. The evidence collected must show that all these criteria are met.

Range statements
These describe the contexts in which you would expect the individual to be able to achieve the standard. Evidence is required which shows that the individual can agree assessment plans in each of the contexts defined by the range.

EVIDENCE REQUIREMENTS	Guidance to assessors of this Element
The performance evidence required:	[additional to the Guidance Notes]
Three assessment plans. Each plan should cover at least two elements and three sources of evidence.	1 The plans should be assessed by examining them (or a copy of them).
The knowledge evidence required:	2 The two elements may be the same for each candidate.
i how to meet candidate's needs for access to fair and reliable assessment in line with the relevant legislation, and how to recognise and eliminate unfair discrimination;	3 Evidence must be gathered that the assessor-candidate can take the needs of candidates into account when planning assessment, including those with little previous experience of assessment, and those with special assessment requirements. If the performance evidence does not show this, check the assessor-candidate's knowledge and understanding.
ii what the different opportunities for evidence collection are and how to evaluate their relevance and appropriateness;	4 Criterion e
When there is a disagreement, options might include: further discussion; postponement of the assessment; seeking another assessor; giving the candidate access to advice from a third party; withdrawal from the assessment process.
iii different types of evidence, their role in assessment and valid ways of collecting them;	
iv how to collect evidence cost effectively and efficiently;	5 Reviews of the assessment plans may be informal or formal. They should not, of course, add so much to the time and costs of the assessment process as to become a barrier to access.
v ways of developing and agreeing assessment plans which are relevant to different types of candidates and their needs;	6 Candidate reports may take different forms, such as diaries and logs. Peer reports may be in the form of witness testimony.
vi how to obtain the agreement of the candidate and others to the assessment plan without this process becoming a barrier to assessment and in ways which offer him/her authentic choice;	7 Evidence gathered for D321 may be relevant to achieving this element. Evidence for this element which relates to plans to judge naturally occurring evidence, and related questioning, may contribute to the evidence for D321.
vii what types of special assessment requirements there are, ways of providing for them and who to approach for advice.	

Performance evidence
This sets out what (and how much) evidence is needed to show that the individual can achieve the element.

Knowledge evidence
This defines what underpinning knowledge the individual should demonstrate. This is frequently apparent in the performance evidence. When it is not, other sources will be needed.

Guidance notes of the element
These add to the guidance given in the general Guidance Notes for Units D32 and D33 presented on the following page. They are intended to help the person assessing performance against this standard.

Guidance Notes for Assessors of Units D32 and D33

1 Performance evidence is needed for each element of competence within each Unit. This should normally be derived from real assessment environments. How much performance evidence is needed is set out in the statement of evidence requirements for each element. The combined performance and knowledge evidence must demonstrate that the assessor-candidate can assess accurately for NCVQ accredited/validated qualifications.

2 When used to collect performance evidence, observations of performance might be directly from being there, or may come by recording the performance, for example on video or audiotape.

3 Evidence must be judged against all the performance criteria in an element. Please note the following guidance:

"To be judged as meeting the national standard, each combination of performance evidence with its supporting evidence must meet all the performance criteria of the element which are relevant to the occasion...... It is not appropriate for a separate piece of evidence to be generated for each individual performance criterion. Not only is 'atomised' evidence of this sort inefficient, it is also often wrong. It only shows that the candidate achieves the standard on a piecemeal basis, rather than being consistently competent to the full national standard."

Source: "Implementing the national standards for assessment and verification" NCVQ 1994

4 If performance evidence cannot be obtained from the individual's current or previous work, look for evidence from alternative sources. If a simulation is used,

  • it must be realistic: that is, it must replicate all the critical factors and conditions to be found in the individual's normal work environment, and specifically those factors and conditions that impinge on achieving the national standard. Simulations which cannot achieve this degree of realism should not be used for assessment purposes;

  • it must allow valid and reliable assessment to the standards needed in employment.

5 You may need to collect supporting evidence (for example of the individual's knowledge and understanding) when the performance evidence does not cover all the categories listed in the range statements.

6 Performance evidence and supporting evidence should be gathered efficiently. For example, you will want a source which can produce several items of evidence, rather than using a different source for each bit of evidence you need. Also, you will want to look for opportunities to gather evidence which is common to several elements. For example, some of the evidence gathered towards D321 may be relevant to D331 as well.

7 How you get supporting evidence may vary to suit the assessor-candidate's circumstances. Here are some sources that may be used:

  • witness testimony from the candidate being assessed.
  • a written log by the assessor-candidate
  • answers to oral questions.
  • written scenarios, or written or oral answers to "What if...?" questions relevant to range categories not fully covered by the performance evidence.

8 You must be confident that the assessor-candidate understands and can apply the knowledge listed in the Knowledge Evidence section of the statement of evidence requirements. Much will be apparent in the performance evidence. Questioning will often clarify the individual's understanding, though you may need to use other methods.

9 Difficulties in meeting the full evidence requirement should be referred to the external verifier for the appropriate awarding body.

10 Equality of access to fair and valid assessment is a guarantee for all candidates for NVQs/GNVQs/units. Evidence that assessor-candidates are capable of providing equality of access and eliminating unfair discrimination is required for each Unit. The standards, evidence requirements and guidance notes identify how this applies in each case.

TRAINING & DEVELOPMENT LEAD BODY
NATIONAL STANDARDS FOR ASSESSMENT & VERIFICATION

D32   ASSESS CANDIDATE PERFORMANCE

Assessment is the process of collecting and judging evidence of a candidate's performance against nationally agreed standards (or "elements of competence").

This Unit specifies what has to be achieved by someone making assessments of a candidate's performance under realistic conditions in the workplace, in a training centre or a college. There are four elements:

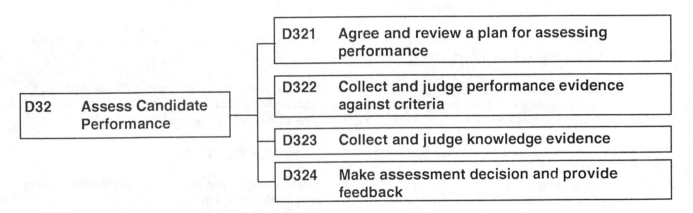

Assessment decisions are a matter of judgement as to whether there is sufficient evidence to conclude that the elements have been achieved. It is, therefore, important that the assessor is able to help the candidate to produce a realistic plan that is likely to generate sufficient evidence of the right quality. In this case, the assessor will be planning to judge evidence that is derived from 'natural performance' - by examining products of the candidate's work, and by observing the candidate in action.

The assessor is also expected to gather evidence of knowledge from performance evidence and by checking for it - for example by using questioning techniques.

All candidates for NVQs, GNVQs and Units are to be given equality of access to fair assessment. When planning assessments, collecting evidence and making assessment decisions, the assessor is expected to clarify and take account of candidates' needs, to provide equality of access, and to act to eliminate unfair discrimination in the assessment process.

Evidence collected for this unit may also contribute to the evidence required for D33, for assessor-candidates wishing to achieve that unit.

PLEASE NOTE: to avoid confusion the term "assessor-candidate" is used to identify the person seeking to achieve this Unit. "Candidate" means the individual assessed by the assessor-candidate.

Unit

D32   Assess Candidate Performance

Element

D321   Agree and review a plan for assessing performance

Performance Criteria

a   the opportunities identified are relevant to the elements to be assessed

b   best use is made of naturally occurring evidence and related questioning

c   opportunities are selected to minimise disruption to normal activity

d   opportunities are selected which provide access to fair and reliable assessment

e   when simulations are proposed, accurate information and advice is sought about their validity and administration

f   the proposed assessment plan is discussed and agreed with the candidate and others who may be affected

g   if there is disagreement with the proposed assessment plan, options open to the candidate are explained clearly and constructively

h   the assessment plan specifies the target elements of competence, the types of evidence to be collected, the assessment methods, the timing of assessments and the arrangements for reviewing progress against the plan

i   plans are reviewed and updated at agreed times to reflect the candidate's progress within the qualification

Range Statements

1   Evidence
Performance evidence; knowledge evidence

2   Evidence derived from
Examination of products; observations of process; responses to questions

3   Opportunities for evidence collection
Naturally occurring; preset simulations and tests;
For candidates with special assessment requirements

EVIDENCE REQUIREMENTS

The performance evidence required:

One assessment plan for one candidate covering at least three elements. The plan should be assessed by examining it (or a copy of it).

The knowledge evidence required:

i   ways of involving different candidates in developing and agreeing assessment plans to meet their needs;

ii   what evidence requirements are, and how to identify relevant evidence from what is actually or potentially available;

iii   what naturally occurring evidence is and why it is important for assessment purposes;

iv   different methods for collecting performance evidence and how to select appropriate, efficient methods;

v   when to use simulations and alternative sources, and from whom to seek advice when simulations and alternative sources are required;

vi   the place of knowledge evidence in assessment and ways of collecting it;

vii   how to meet candidate's needs for access to fair and reliable assessment in line with the relevant legislation, and how to recognise and eliminate unfair discrimination;

viii   what types of special assessment requirements there are, ways of providing for them and who to approach for advice.

Guidance for assessors of this element

1   *The three elements may be in the same or different Units of Competence.*

2   *You must have evidence that the assessor-candidate can identify and plan for equal access to fair assessment. This includes how to make arrangements for equal access for those with special assessment requirements. If the performance evidence does not reveal this, check the assessor-candidate's knowledge and understanding.*

3   *Criterion g*
When there is a disagreement, options might include: further discussion: postponement of the assessment; seeking another assessor: giving the candidate access to advice from a third party; withdrawal from the assessment process.

4   *Criterion e*
The assessor-candidate is not expected to be able to design simulations. When these are necessary, the assessor-candidate is expected to seek accurate information and advice (from, for example, their verifier) about relevant simulations. The extent to which the assessor-candidate needs to seek information and advice will, of course, vary according to the circumstances.

5   *Evidence provided for this element may contribute towards achievement of D331, and some of the evidence produced for D331 may contribute towards achievement of this element.*

6   *Reviews of the assessment plans may be informal or formal. They should not add so much to the time and costs of the assessment process as to become a barrier to access.*

Unit

D32   Assess Candidate Performance

Element

D322   Collect and judge performance evidence against criteria

Performance Criteria

a   advice and encouragement to collect evidence efficiently is appropriate to the candidate's needs

b   access to assessment is appropriate to the candidate's needs

c   only the performance criteria specified for the element of competence are used to judge the evidence

d   evidence is judged accurately against all the relevant performance criteria

e   the evidence is valid and can be attributed to the candidate

f   any preset simulations and tests are administered correctly

g   the assessor is as unobtrusive as is practicable whilst observing the candidate

h   evidence is judged fairly and reliably

i   difficulties in judging evidence fairly and reliably are referred promptly to an appropriate authority

j   the candidate is given clear and constructive feedback and advice following the judgement

Range Statements

1   Performance evidence assessed by
Examination of products; observations of process

2   Candidates
Experienced in presenting evidence; inexperienced in presenting evidence
Candidates with special assessment requirements

EVIDENCE REQUIREMENTS

The performance evidence required:

A   Judgements of performance against at least three elements. Each judgement must be made against all the relevant performance criteria in the element;

B   The way the assessor-candidate collects evidence, makes the judgements and provides feedback (formal or informal).

The knowledge evidence required:

i   ways of encouraging candidates with differing levels of confidence and experience to take an active part in their assessment in such a way that this does not in itself inhibit them or hinder access to assessment;

ii   different candidate's needs and their relevance to providing access to fair and reliable assessment;

iii   what national standards are and how to judge evidence against them fairly and reliably;

iv   what evidence requirements are and how to identify relevant evidence from what is available;

v   why it is important to make an accurate judgement against all the relevant criteria in an element;

vi   why it is important to make an accurate judgement against only the criteria specified nationally for certification;

vii   ways of checking the validity and, particularly for product evidence, authenticity of evidence;

viii   how to administer preset simulations and tests;

ix   how to collect evidence unobtrusively by observation;

x   types of difficulty which may occur in making fair and reliable judgements of evidence;

xi   who to approach within the local and national system when there are difficulties;

xii   what types of special assessment requirements there are, ways of providing for them, and who to approach for advice

---

Guidance to assessors of this element

[additional to the Guidance Notes]

1   *The performance evidence may relate to the same candidate with whom the assessment plan is agreed in D321.*

2   *Performance criteria (f) and (i) describe situations that may not arise when judging performance. When this is the case, look for evidence that the assessor-candidate understands how to administer preset simulations correctly and/or understands what to do when faced with difficulties in judging evidence.*

3   *"Unobtrusive" means (1) the observation does not so affect the candidate's performance that it influences the outcome, and (2) the assessor-candidate's presence does not disrupt or disturb what others maybe doing in the assessment context.*

4   *Evidence provided for this element may contribute towards achievement of D332, and some of the evidence produced for D332 may contribute towards achievement of this element.*

D32 Assess Candidate Performance

Element

D323   Collect and judge knowledge evidence

Performance Criteria

a   knowledge relevant to the element is identified accurately from the performance evidence

b   evidence of knowledge is collected when performance evidence does not cover fully the specified range or contingencies

c   valid methods are used to collect knowledge evidence

d   when questions are used, they are clear and do not lead candidates

e   access to assessment is appropriate to the candidate's needs

f   the knowledge evidence conforms with the content of the knowledge specification and is judged accurately against all the relevant performance criteria

g   evidence is judged fairly and reliably

h   difficulties in judging evidence fairly and reliably are referred promptly to an appropriate authority

i   the candidate is given clear and constructive feedback and advice following the judgement

Range Statements

1   Knowledge evidence derived from
Examination of product(s); observation(s) of process; responses to questions

2   Candidates
Experienced in presenting evidence; inexperienced in presenting evidence
Candidates with special assessment requirements

3   Questions
Oral; written
Preset questions; assessor devised questions

EVIDENCE REQUIREMENTS:

The performance evidence required:

A   Records of oral or written questions devised by the assessor-candidate for at least one candidate, covering knowledge evidence in relation to at least three elements of competence, and how the validity and reliability of the questions was checked;

B   The way the assessor-candidate collects and judges knowledge evidence relevant to at least three elements, and provides feedback (formal or informal).

The knowledge evidence required:

i   the role of knowledge in assessment, what the knowledge evidence requirements are, and how to identify relevant evidence from available performance evidence;

ii   why it is important to collect evidence related to contingencies and across the specified range, and ways of doing this;

iii   what the available sources of knowledge evidence are and how to use them;

iv   how to administer any preset tests and questions;

v   how to frame, adapt and ask questions which will elicit relevant and valid evidence whilst maintaining the candidate's confidence;

vi   how to judge knowledge evidence fairly and reliably;

vii   common difficulties that may arise in collecting and assessing knowledge evidence;

viii   how to provide access to candidates with special assessment requirements;

ix   who to approach within the local and national system when there are difficulties.

Guidance to assessors of this element

[additional to the Guidance Notes]

1   *The performance evidence is in two parts. This evidence may relate to the same candidate.*

2   *Performance criterion (b) describes a situation that may not arise when you collect performance evidence. When this happens, use questioning or other methods to check the assessor-candidate's understanding of what to do to ensure coverage of the range, contingencies and underpinning knowledge.*

3   *Evidence provided for this element may contribute towards achievement of D332, and some of the evidence produced for D332 may contribute towards achievement of this element.*

4   *The validity and reliability of questions can be checked, for example:*

   • *against samples of expected answers*
   • *with subject specialists*
   • *with verifiers*
   • *with colleagues*

Unit

D32 **Assess Candidate Performance**

Element

D324 **Make assessment decision and provide feedback**

Performance Criteria

a the decision is based on all the relevant performance and knowledge evidence available

b when the combined evidence is sufficient to cover the range, the performance criteria and the evidence specification, the candidate is informed of his/her achievement

c when evidence is insufficient, the candidate is given a clear explanation and appropriate advice

d feedback following the decision is clear, constructive, meets the candidate's needs and is appropriate to his/her level of confidence

e the candidate is encouraged to seek clarification and advice

f evidence and assessment decisions are recorded to meet verification requirements

g records are legible and accurate, are stored securely and are passed on to the next stage of the recording/certification process promptly

Range Statements

1 Records of
Assessment decisions; evidence

2 Candidates
Experienced in presenting evidence; inexperienced in presenting evidence
Candidates with special assessment requirements

3 Sufficiency of evidence
Sufficient to make the decision; insufficient to make the decision

4 Evidence derived from
Examination of products; observations of process; responses to questions

---

EVIDENCE REQUIREMENTS

The performance evidence required:

A **Records of assessment evidence and decisions for one candidate related to at least three elements of competence;**

and

B **The way the assessor-candidate gives feedback to one candidate.**

The candidate referred to in (A) and (B) need not be the same person.

The knowledge evidence required:

i what standards are and how to assess fairly and reliably against them;

ii how to give constructive feedback to candidates according to the nature of the decision taken;

iii how to adapt feedback to differing levels of confidence and experience in candidates;

iv different types of advice and how to offer it constructively and in ways that allow candidates choice;

v how to encourage candidates to ask questions and seek advice;

vi how to record and process assessment decisions;

vii what the requirements of the verification process are.

Guidance to assessors of this element

[additional to the Guidance Notes]

1 *The performance evidence required in (B) would normally be collected by observation of the assessor-candidate giving feedback. A role play would not be acceptable as a means of generating evidence.*

2 *Evidence must be gathered that the assessor-candidate can make fair decisions and give constructive feedback which is sensitive to candidates with differing degrees of self-confidence. If you do not find sufficient evidence in the performance evidence, use questioning to check the assessor-candidate's knowledge and understanding.*

3 *Criterion (c) describes a situation that may not arise in the performance evidence. When this is the case, check the assessor-candidate's knowledge and understanding of how to give feedback when evidence is insufficient to infer competence.*

4 *Evidence produced for this element may contribute towards achievement of D333, and evidence produced for D333 may be relevant to achieving this element.*

TRAINING & DEVELOPMENT LEAD BODY
NATIONAL STANDARDS FOR ASSESSMENT & VERIFICATION

D33 ASSESS CANDIDATE USING DIFFERING SOURCES OF EVIDENCE

This Unit specifies national standards for the assessor who has to collect and judge evidence of competence from a variety of sources. These will include the judgements of evidence provided by others, the candidate and the candidate's peers. They will also include assessments of prior achievements and the outcomes of assessments of performance covered in D32.

The Unit has three elements:

	D331	**Agree and review an assessment plan**
D33 Assess Candidate Using Differing Sources of Evidence	**D332**	**Judge evidence and provide feedback**
	D333	**Make assessment decision using differing sources of evidence and provide feedback**

These describe the outcomes a competent assessor should achieve at each stage in the process of assessing evidence from a variety of sources. The evidence must be that associated with the element being assessed and must meet the requirements for sufficiency laid down by the appropriate Lead Body and by the Awarding Body.

Assessment decisions are a matter of judgement as to whether there is sufficient evidence to conclude that the elements have been achieved. It is, therefore, important that the assessor is able to agree a realistic plan that is likely to generate sufficient evidence of the right quality from all the available sources. It is equally important that the plan incorporates efficient evidence collection. This includes examining the potential each source may have for generating evidence relevant to several elements. Candidate participation in the process is to be encouraged, though the assessor should avoid arrangements that are either so time-consuming, bureaucratic, or daunting for the candidate, that they impede access to assessment.

All candidates for NVQs, GNVQs and Units are to be given equality of access to fair assessment. When planning assessments, judging evidence and making assessment decisions, the assessor is expected to assess and take account of candidates' needs, to provide equality of access, and to act to eliminate unfair discrimination in the assessment process.

Some of the evidence required for this unit may also be relevant to D32, for assessor-candidates wishing to achieve that unit.

PLEASE NOTE: to avoid confusion the term "assessor-candidate" is used to identify the person seeking to achieve this Unit. "Candidate" means the individual assessed by the assessor-candidate.

Unit

D33 Assess Candidate Using Differing Sources of Evidence

Element

D331 Agree and review an assessment plan

Performance Criteria

a possible opportunities for collecting evidence are identified and evaluated against their relevance to the element(s) to be assessed and their appropriateness to the candidate's needs

b evidence collection is planned to make effective use of time and resources

c the opportunities selected provide access to fair and reliable assessment

d the proposed assessment plan is discussed and agreed with the candidate and others who may be affected

e if there is disagreement with the proposed assessment plan, options open to the candidate are explained clearly and constructively

f the assessment plan specifies the target element(s), the opportunities for efficient evidence collection, the assessment methods, the timing of assessments and the arrangements for reviewing the plan

g requirements to assure the authenticity, reliability and sufficiency of evidence are identified

h plans are reviewed and updated at agreed times to reflect the candidate's progress within the qualification

Range Statements

1 Opportunities for collecting evidence from

Natural performance; simulations; projects and assignments; questioning; candidate and peer reports; candidate's prior achievement and learning

2 Evidence used for

Own judgements; judgements by other people

3 Candidates

Experienced in presenting evidence; inexperienced in presenting evidence

Candidates with special assessment requirements

EVIDENCE REQUIREMENTS

The performance evidence required:

Three assessment plans. Each plan should cover at least two elements and three sources of evidence.

The knowledge evidence required:

i how to meet candidate's needs for access to fair and reliable assessment in line with the relevant legislation, and how to recognise and eliminate unfair discrimination;

ii what the different opportunities for evidence collection are and how to evaluate their relevance and appropriateness;

iii different types of evidence, their role in assessment and valid ways of collecting them;

iv how to collect evidence cost effectively and efficiently;

v ways of developing and agreeing assessment plans which are relevant to different types of candidates and their needs;

vi how to obtain the agreement of the candidate and others to the assessment plan without this process becoming a barrier to assessment and in ways which offer him/her authentic choice;

vii what types of special assessment requirements there are, ways of providing for them and who to approach for advice.

Guidance to assessors of this element

[additional to the Guidance Notes]

1 *The plans should be assessed by examining them (or a copy of them).*

2 *The two elements may be the same for each candidate.*

3 *Evidence must be gathered that the assessor-candidate can take the needs of candidates into account when planning assessment, including those with little previous experience of assessment, and those with special assessment requirements. If the performance evidence does not show this, check the assessor-candidate's knowledge and understanding.*

4 *Criterion e*
When there is a disagreement, options might include: further discussion; postponement of the assessment; seeking another assessor; giving the candidate access to advice from a third party; withdrawal from the assessment process.

5 *Reviews of the assessment plans may be informal or formal. They should not, of course, add so much to the time and costs of the assessment process as to become a barrier to access.*

6 *Candidate reports may take different forms, such as diaries and logs. Peer reports may be in the form of witness testimony.*

7 *Evidence gathered for D321 may be relevant to achieving this element. Evidence for this element, which relates to plans to plans to judge naturally occurring evidence, and related questioning, may contribute to the evidence for D321.*

Unit

D33 Assess Candidate Using Differing Sources of Evidence

Element

D332 Judge evidence and provide feedback

Performance Criteria

a advice and encouragement to collect evidence efficiently is appropriate to the candidate's needs

b access to assessment is appropriate to the candidate's needs

c the evidence is valid and can be attributed to the candidate

d only the criteria specified for the element are used to judge the evidence

e evidence is judged accurately against all the relevant performance criteria

f when evidence of prior achievement/learning is used, checks are made that the candidate can currently achieve the relevant national standard

g evidence is judged fairly and reliably

h difficulties in authenticating and judging evidence are referred to the appropriate authority promptly

i when evidence is not to the national standard, the candidate is given a clear explanation and appropriate advice

j feedback following the decision is clear, constructive, meets the candidate's needs and is appropriate to his/her level of confidence

Range Statements

1 Evidence derived from

Natural performance; simulations; projects and assignments; questioning; candidate and peer reports; candidate's prior achievement and learning

2 Evidence used for

Own judgements; judgements by other people

3 Candidates

Experienced in presenting evidence; inexperienced in presenting evidence
Candidates with special assessment requirements

EVIDENCE REQUIREMENTS

The performance evidence required:

In respect of six judgements of evidence, covering overall three or more sources (described in Range 1):

A Records of evidence considered and judgements made;

and

B The way the assessor-candidate makes the judgements and provides feedback (formal or informal)

The knowledge evidence required:

i ways of encouraging candidates with differing levels of confidence and experience to take an active part in their assessment in such a way that this does not in itself inhibit them or hinder access to assessment;

ii different candidate's needs and their relevance to providing access to fair and reliable assessment;

iii what national standards are and how to judge evidence against them fairly and reliably;

iv what evidence requirements are and how to identify relevant evidence from what is available;

v why it is important to make an accurate judgement against all the relevant criteria in an element;

vi why it is important to make an accurate judgement against only the criteria specified nationally for certification;

vii ways of checking the validity and authenticity of evidence, particularly product evidence;

viii how to administer preset simulations and tests;

ix how to collect evidence unobtrusively by observation;

x types of difficulty which may occur in making fair and reliable judgements of evidence;

xi who to approach within the local and national system when there are difficulties;

xii what types of special assessment requirements there are, ways of providing for them, and who to approach for advice;

xiii what the differing sources of evidence are and how to use them to provide the required evidence.

Guidance to assessors of this element

[additional to the Guidance Notes]

1 *Performance criteria (f) and (h) describe a situation that may not arise in the performance evidence. When this is the case, check the assessor-candidate's knowledge and understanding of how to recognise and deal with inconsistencies and other difficulties, and how to check that candidates can currently achieve the national standard.*

2 *You must be confident that the assessor-candidate understands and can apply the knowledge listed opposite. In particular, you may need to check the assessor-candidate's knowledge and understanding of how to make fair and reliable criterion-referenced judgements, and how this knowledge has been used in the cases presented as evidence.*

3 *Evidence gathered for D322 and D323 may be relevant to achieving this element. Evidence for this element relating to the judgement of naturally occurring evidence, and related questioning, may contribute to the evidence for D322/D323.*

4 *It is not necessary for the judgements to be related to the plans submitted for D331.*

Unit

D33 Assess Candidate Using Differing Sources of Evidence

Element

D333 Make assessment decision using differing sources of evidence and provide feedback

Performance Criteria

a the decision is based on all relevant evidence available

b any inconsistencies in the evidence are clarified and resolved

c when the combined evidence is sufficient to cover the range, the performance criteria and the evidence specification, the candidate is informed of his/her achievement

d when evidence is insufficient, the candidate is given a clear explanation and appropriate advice

e feedback following the decision is clear, constructive, meets the candidate's needs and is appropriate to his/her level of confidence

f the candidate is encouraged to seek clarification and advice

g evidence and assessment decisions are recorded to meet verification requirements

h records are legible and accurate, stored securely and passed to the next stage of recording/certification process promptly

Range Statements

1 Records of

Assessment decisions; evidence

2 Candidates

Experienced in presenting evidence; inexperienced in presenting evidence

Candidates with special assessment requirements

3 Evidence

Sufficient to make decision; insufficient to make decision

Own judgements; judgements made by other people

4 Evidence derived from

Natural performance; simulations; projects and assignments; questioning; candidate and peer reports; candidate's prior achievement and learning

EVIDENCE REQUIREMENTS

The performance evidence required:

A Records of assessment evidence and decisions related to at least two elements;

and

B The way the assessor-candidate gives feedback to one candidate.

The candidate referred to in (A) and (B) need not be the same person.

The knowledge evidence required:

i what standards are and how to assess fairly and reliably against them;

ii what evidence is available and how to assess fairly and reliably;

iii how to make consistent assessment decisions;

iv how to give constructive feedback to candidates according to the nature of the decision taken;

v how to adapt feedback to differing levels of confidence and experience in candidates;

vi different types of advice and how to offer it constructively and in ways that allow candidates choice;

vii how to encourage candidates to ask questions and seek advice;

viii how to record and process assessment decisions;

ix what the requirements of the verification process are.

1 *The way the assessor-candidate adapts feedback to the needs and sensitivities of the candidate is critical - hence the evidence required in (B). This would normally be collected through observation of the assessor-candidate. Evidence from role plays will not be sufficient.*

2 *Evidence must be gathered that the assessor-candidate can make fair decisions and give constructive feedback to candidates with differing levels of confidence. When this is not apparent in the performance evidence, check the assessor-candidate's knowledge and understanding.*

3 *Performance criterion (d) describes a situation that may not arise in the performance evidence. When this is the case, check the assessor-candidate's knowledge and understanding of what to do when further evidence is needed, for example, from:-*

- *witness testimony from candidates receiving advice;*
- *a written log of advice and support kept by the assessor-candidate;*
- *answers to oral questions.*

4 *Evidence gathered for D324 may be relevant to achieving this element. Evidence for this element relating to plans for assessment and feedback of performance may contribute to the evidence for D324*

Appendix 2 Self-assessment and planning how to use the workbook

The documents in this appendix are designed to illustrate how to carry out self-assessment against the units you need in the TDLB standards. Having completed this self-assessment you will be able to plan how best to use the workbook.

Before doing this, it might be helpful to read Chapters 1, 2, 3 and 4. There is an example of self-assessment in Chapter 11.

The first step is to complete the self-assessment sheets for the unit/s you require.

For each element in the TDLB units tick the column or columns which best describe your situation. Units D32 and D33 include similar activities. If you are planning to cover both units, concentrate on the scope and detail in unit D33 and most of the requirements for D32 will be covered.

An example of a self-assessment form is given in Chapter 11 where a candidate for the administration NVQs completed a self-assessment for unit L1.5.

When you tick column A or D

For elements where your self-assessment lies in column A or D you will probably not need to study the relevant section in the workbook in great detail. A quick read-through will be sufficient. The exercises in the text will give you the opportunity to practise and confirm your skills and provide evidence for your portfolio. You can identify the exercises to do on the planning sheet.

When you tick column B or E

For elements where your self-assessment lies in column B or E you will probably want to go through the relevant section in the workbook thoroughly. This will allow you to check your knowledge and develop your learning. Doing the exercises in these sections will consolidate that learning and build your confidence. You can identify the relevant sections and exercises on the planning sheet.

When you tick column C

For elements where you tick column C you will need to study the relevant sections in the workbook and carry out the exercises and assignments to consolidate your learning. Enter dates on the planning sheet when you will do this.

Study plan

When you have completed your self-assessment sheet/s and entered your decisions on the planning sheet in this appendix you will have a plan on how to use the workbook. This will help to discipline your studies.

Name		Organisation

Unit title:	Date:	Unit No.: D32

Assess candidate performance

Unit topics

Basic principles of NVQ and/or GNVQ assessment
The types and sources of evidence
Evidence requirements
Quality criteria for evidence
Different candidates' needs and how to adapt the
assessment process to provide fair and reliable assessment
Assessment plans
Observing candidates
Questioning techniques to infer knowledge
Giving feedback
Documentation to record assessment
Necessary advice and support from the Internal Verifier
Advice, support and fairness to the candidate

Examples of evidence

Assessment plans negotiated with candidates
List of questions to ask
How questions meet criteria
Assessment records
Candidate-assessor reflective report
Observation of assessor's performance in:
● Assessment planning
● Assessing by observation
● Questioning
● Judging evidence
● Giving feedback

Elements	A	B	C	D	E
D321 Agree and review a plan for assessing performance					
D322 Collect and judge performance evidence against criteria					
D323 Collect and judge knowledge evidence					
D324 Make assessment decision and provide feedback					

LEGEND

A - I do this now as part of my work and, according to the standards, can identify evidence of my competence.

B - I do this now but either I am unsure of my competence or I am unsure of gathering evidence.

C - I am unsure how to do this work activity.

D - I have done this in the past and can offer evidence of recent performance according to the standards.

E - I have done this in the past and feel confident of my ability but I am unsure of gathering evidence.

Possible strategies

Gather evidence and present to the assessor - probably supported by observation of performance.

Support and advice in identifying and gathering evidence supplemented by observation of performance.

Plan training and development.

Gather evidence and present to assessor. Make plans for the assessment of present performance.

Support and advice in identifying and gathering evidence supplemented by observation of performance.

Name	Organisation

Unit title:	Date:	Unit No.: D33

Assess candidate using differing sources of evidence

Unit topics

Basic principles of NVQ and/or GNVQ assessment

The types and sources of evidence: observation of natural performance, simulations, projects, assignments, candidate and peer reports and candidate's prior achievement

Evidence requirements

Quality criteria for evidence

Different candidate's needs and how to adapt the assessment process to provide fair and reliable assessment

Assessment plans

Observing candidates

Questioning techniques to infer knowledge

Giving feedback

Documentation to record assessment

Necessary advice and support from the Internal Verifier

Advice, support and fairness to the candidate

Examples of evidence

Assessment plans negotiated with candidates

List of questions to ask

How questions meet criteria

Assessment records

Candidates reflective report

Observation of assessor's performance in:
- Assessment planning
- Assessing by observation
- Questioning
- Judging evidence
- Giving feedback

Elements	A	B	C	D	E
D331 Agree and review an assessment plan					
D332 Judge evidence and provide feedback					
D333 Make assessment decision using differing sources of evidence and provide feedback					

LEGEND

A - I do this now as part of my work and, according to the standards, can identify evidence of my competence.

B - I do this now but either I am unsure of my competence or I am unsure of gathering evidence.

C - I am unsure how to do this work activity.

D - I have done this in the past and can offer evidence of recent performance according to the standards.

E - I have done this in the past and feel confident of my ability but I am unsure of gathering evidence.

Possible strategies

Gather evidence and present to the assessor - probably supported by observation of performance.

Support and advice in identifying and gathering evidence supplemented by observation of performance.

Plan training and development.

Gather evidence and present to assessor. Make plans for the assessment of present performance.

Support and advice in identifying and gathering evidence supplemented by observation of performance.

PLAN OF WORKBOOK CONTENT AND EXERCISES

Chapter / section in the workbook	TDLB elements covered by the chapter	Plan to read the text	Plan to complete exercises
Who are assessors? Chapter 1	background information		
Part of the assessment team Chapter 2	background information		
The basis of assessment Chapter 3	background information		
Explaining national standards Chapter 4	321, 331		
Identifying and recognising evidence Chapter 5	321, 331		
Judging evidence Chapter 6	322, 323, 324, 332, 333		
Observing performance Chapter 7	322, 332		
Questioning candidates and others Chapter 8	323, 332		
Giving feedback Chapter 9	324, 332, 333		
Recording Chapter 10	324, 333		
Worked example, NVQ Chapter 11	all		
Worked example, GNVQ Chapter 12	all		

After completing your self-assessment(s) decide which sections in the workbook you need to use. Put a start date in the text column.

If you plan to do the exercises, put a starting date in the column.

Appendix 3 Portfolio: structure, details and pro-formas

This appendix gives guidance on how to build your portfolio as an assessor. You will need to do this if you are aiming to achieve the TDLB units. The principles of portfolio building presented here are useful for any competence-based portfolio.

What is a portfolio?

A portfolio can be a folder, box, shelf or pile of paper.

It provides the evidence of your performance in relation to a set of standards in an accessible, structured form.

It has sections to include:

○ information about you - personal details

○ a brief résumé of previous and present work experience

○ a set of standards

○ a place to keep evidence.

Evidence presented in the portfolio needs to be structured in a way that make sense to the candidate, whose portfolio it is, and shows their assessor how the evidence is related to the standards.

There are many ways of structuring your portfolio.

It is important for you to find a way that makes sense for you and shows clearly:

○ **what evidence you have collected**

○ **how you have matched that evidence to the requirements of the standards.**

Collecting the evidence

Keep each item of evidence separately and give it a reference number. At this stage don't worry about how the item of evidence relates particularly to the standards or its order in the referencing system.

Plastic pockets are useful to keep items of evidence.

When you have a number of items of evidence complete an evidence summary sheet for each element (see example on next page).

On the summary sheet list each item of evidence that is relevant to that element and relate it to the relevant performance criterion by a tick in the appropriate column. A piece of evidence may well be relevant to a number of performance criteria across a number of elements. You should also show which aspects of the range have been covered in the right-hand column.

At any stage you will also be able to check that you have sufficient evidence which covers all the performance criteria in an element. An assessor will also be able to see if you have covered all the performance criteria.

The sheet on the next page shows an example of a completed summary sheet for D331. This example covers all the performance criteria, across the range.

Evidence summary sheet

Unit no. and title: *D33 Assess candidate using differing sources of evidence*

Element no. and title:

D331 Agree and review an assessment plan

Performance criteria in element

Use numbers or letters from the standards

Evidence ref. and description	a	b	c	d	e	f	g	h			Reference item of evidence to the range
1. Six assessment plans	✔	✔	✔	✔		✔					covers all the range
2. Log of review meetings	✔			✔	✔	✔		✔			covers all types of candidates
6. Testimony from my candidate		✔	✔	✔	✔						special assessment requirements
7. Self-report on quality criteria	✔						✔				covers all the range
12. Self-report on assessment planning	✔	✔	✔			✔		✔			covers all the range

Start by referencing the evidence that is relevant to this element with a number. List this evidence in the left-hand column and tick the performance criteria columns that are covered by that particular piece of evidence. In the last column, note how the piece of evidence applies to the range statements in the element. Once referenced, evidence can be used for other elements in the same way.

You can use as many sheets as you need and may wish to present them at the beginning of the element in your portfolio.

This sheet is designed to show what sort of details you might include as information about yourself. Awarding bodies often issue registration forms and these can kept at the front of your portfolio as an official form.

Personal details

(Name)

(Address)

(Employer/approved centre)

(Employer's/approved centre address)

(Phone)

(Fax)

(Qualification/award)

(Awarding body)

(Awarding body registration number)

(Name of assessor contact - phone and/or address)

Brief work résumé

This is not a curriculum vitae. It should not include all your experience and qualifications. The résumé should present experience relevant to the standards in the portfolio. In the case of the TDLB standards this might be assessment experience, supervisory experience, training courses or qualifications you have got.

The purpose of this résumé is to help you link your experience to your present competence and to identify possible sources of evidence from that experience. The résumé will help your assessor get a picture of your experience.

This résumé can include experiences outside work if they are relevant to the standards in this portfolio and have contributed to the development of your competence.

Start with your most recent experience. For each period of time give details of the experience as it relates to the standards in this portfolio.

Do not list everything you did, but concentrate on identifying what is relevant to the standards.

The completed example below will illustrate what to include.

DATES	DETAIL OF EXPERIENCE AS IT RELATES TO THE STANDARDS
	Include any contact information of supervisors, colleagues, trainers and lecturers who may be willing to provide evidence of previous experience.
Oct '93 to present	*Took part in a pilot exercise in my organisation looking at using NVQs in cleaning. Trained and practised as an assessor with two candidates. Contributed to assessor meetings and feedback on how the assessments were going. Kept records and reports throughout this time.*
Feb '93	*Attended supervisor training which included team-building and giving feedback. Notes and exercises from the course may provide evidence for D324 and D333.*
July '92 to present	*Employed as departmental supervisor. Involved allocation and monitoring of work and performance in a team of ten. Although not involved in direct assessment there was a lot of supervision which cover activities in the standards, like planning, judging and giving feedback.*